Society Awaken
BOOK 2

Millionsof us have yet to Awaken to the destruction
of an easy thing such as drink/drug-driving.

JD. RODRIGUEZ

ISBN 978-93-5458-408-4
© JD. RODRIGUEZ 2021
Published in India 2021 by Pencil

A brand of
One Point Six Technologies Pvt. Ltd.
123, Building J2, Shram Seva Premises,
Wadala Truck Terminal, Wadala (E)
Mumbai 400037, Maharashtra, INDIA
E connect@thepencilapp.com
W www.thepencilapp.com

Author biography

Catastrophe was always on the table, unfamiliar territory has decades in learned new adjendars. From naivitee he went the long tricky path to reveal purpose. Much is learned and new moral and considerations gained. Not much Psychological or academic training but his work is said to be of masters level.

A knowledgable look at growing up troubles and what they can lead to, adolescence was hard, difficulty meant my assumption was life is unfair.

This book contains throughout a receptives view on parenting.

We move onto drunk drive consequences and definate deterrals, as a public speaker on the subject hardened offenders have even admitted to never practicing this ridicule again and sinceirly thanked me for helping them realise.

Including disability acceptances and denials, again from a receptive insider view of societal attitudes and accepted inclusion.

This book is a great gift to those you love, teach or support and will without doubt cause a drop in the amount of offenders, injuries and deaths

An insight into equalities, disability, anti drunk driving, society, mind and Divinity.

Catastrophe was always on the table, unfamiliar territory has decades in learned new adjendars. From naivitee he went the long tricky path to reveal purpose. Much is learned and new moral and considerations gained. Not much Psychological or academic training but his work is said to be of masters level.

A knowledgable look at growing up troubles and what they can lead to, adolescence was hard, difficulty meant my assumption was life is unfair.

This book contains throughout a receptives view on parenting.

We move onto drunk drive consequences and definate deterrals, as a public speaker on the subject hardened offenders have even admitted to never practicing this ridicule again and sinceirly thanked me for helping them realise.

Including disability acceptances and denials, again from a receptive insider view of societal attitudes and accepted inclusion.

This book is a great gift to those you love, teach or support and will without doubt cause a drop in the amount of offenders, injuries and deaths

An insight into equalities, disability, anti drunk driving, society, mind and Divinity.

CONTENTS

SECOND HALF OF BOOK

Presence remains always and leads me in the right direction

Suspicion

Was made that way, but was suspicious at the events that seemed too good so denied them and was not overly suspicious at thought that I assumed were connected to memory, I should have been.

I was advised in wrongful deeds, advised of a good provider, then much later another memory, do not use this provider, please things are easier than they are being made, why do this?

Was made paranoid for needless reason, they need not have informed me of irrelevant occurrence that I would otherwise have taken as normal.

There is much in each category, including what I wrote once, which was just to teach others, not a fact I wanted to materialize. which reminds me of something else I wrote. which reminds me of something I witnessed, so this is truth, never utter a word if it is not the whole truth, negative in any way, for another purpose, not what you really want. should i continue? There is so much how the .. am i supposed to operate?

Had to try a different vocabulary, altering even thought, do you know how difficult that is? What is inbred is natural, thought myself was a known self, if i am so known why did all this be allowed to continue? On the meagre hope that what you knew you knew was not truth and the opposite might materialize. so then, no one but no one ever really knows truth ay, do not deny me, I know what I know what you think you know but NO ONE and NO BODY ever knows truth, I maintain hope and faith in the one and only one.

Your stories

Your voices heard

Here we begin an interactive experience, am interested and think this valuable to gain your opinions, stories and lessons.

Please add to my endeavour.

Mr.Pratt.

Shall start us going: One man put his car into the garage wall with his 3- and 4-year-olds in the car after he'd been drinking. Terrifying he said, he burned his license and refuses to drive again. He still likes a drink but respect to him. Thanks for sharing. He concluded this could have ended a nastier way, this scared me to sense.

I asked him for anonymity reasons, what name shall we give you? He quickly replied, pratt! Because I were at the time, now I've got my Grandkids the incident sends shivers, possible I would never have had the chance.

But there is always a vital, he said I would never drink and drive. He does not even drive but if he did. Unless I had to, kids come first, if they were in trouble I would get behind the wheel if could not get a lift. This is all very well but they could be in real trouble if he picked them up then hits a tree on the way home!

Mitch.

Drunk-driving destroyed a friendship my best friendship, many, most, no ALL my friendships! Did not have any lifelong mates because of relocation but had some good mates.

Loss of identity made me a different person to who they made friends with, plus I was confused, vulnerable and easily aggravated.

Started over, had to find a different calibre of mate, which was not a bad thing. They had to be more understanding and patient.

Believe me or not but I had some of my most valuable experiences and meetings since the accident where I grew the most, although I think that is because my perceptions were so changed from living a new reality after disability inducing.

Thanks for that revealing story Mitch.

Man on bench

This was a quick chat; he was enjoying the sunshine while eating his lunch. Simply outlined my purpose and history and asked him what he thought of drunk-drivers.

He said: Do ya want the honest answer, (He started by swearing) then grow up!

Replied yeah but some people especially a young generation think they are invincible so I am educating, even older generations can still drink drive. He responded this should not be about education more about using your common sense. Yes, but we require some educating to enable that because unfortunately some will refrain from sense and still be misguided in treacherous pursuits. Do not entirely agree here, this is all about educating no matter your age, the next comment agrees.

Thanks for your time.

My good friend, call him Jack

Simply says just by knowing ya, witnessing and getting told stories of what you went through have made sure, I will never drink drive for sure!

You can comprehend simple education can be just exposure, no lesson just familiarization to another's experience, this is why speaking to audiences about my challenges of past is powerful, though am changing tact not to come over so whingey. Witnessing my life is such a powerful tool in delivery and fixing messages in the front of mind.

Thanks, I really respect his knowledge and words
We still have a way to go

This is a story of something that I experienced yesterday.

Made a poster that I thought carried a strong message, they all do but this one was different somehow.

I had been awake the full night working on various things and for other reasons so felt a bit groggy but I was so enthused I printed many copies and went to distribute, went in one pub, the perfect places to promote anti drink-driving. Spoke to the girl behind the bar just said have a look at this and decide if it is something you can put up.

She started, got half-way, soon as she viewed mental health, she said oh no, no sorry your ok thanks anyway.

I left got to another place then parked my scooter, had the thought then walked all the way back and said it is the

#ommunity you should be apologising to this is a pub do you not get drunk drivers in.

She blushed and attempted to justify her response, as it happens, they cannot advertise anything unless the head office says so, another girl had said. Should have replied yeah so run it by head office.

I am sure they will not be so naÃ¯ve.

If we still have people of that calibre in the world, then there is certainly drunk drivers and disability prejudice, she displayed part of this.

We still have a long way to go in resolution, the more that assist me the quicker we shall get there.

Am not whinging complaining so much. Have simply found it one of the most effective tools to use to deter others from doing the same. No one wants disability, you can all comprehend where I am coming from, I know how I used to feel when looking at a person with a disability and know most of the population feel the same way.

All forces invisible and the like should be taken into consideration.

A realization: this is slow going. Just want to emphasize the scale of work and determination, all be it unskilled that have gone into a calling. This is a demonstration of will and great obstacle climbing, internal and external, recovery and realized life, mystical and evolutional.

While this writing goes on and while at times I peak and visualize my future as a success, I am not totally content. I feel I am making errors mystical in nature I will not go into detail but just know I am going through trials at present, no matter how I sound. The mammoth failing that so hindered me affected everything, so still I question what I do, how I do it, when I do. I was foretold a future that burdens every move, every thought. So do not think I am on an ego trip and living in cuckoo land, I am demonstrating willpower of kinds, not to be defeated, to ignore if necessary if deterrents do not allow my plan to emerge, and still aim for my goals.

My metaphorical speak of hero and enemy. My or my own influenced thoughts are just some. You see I am in a battle to conceive a destination. I have, no they are not always an enemy but since the turning point, they have certainly made me aware of their presence. Now I do not know whether these are human malfunctions or mystical, I suspect the most, they are humans with mystical qualities. Whatever but I am still not convinced if they are trying to make difficulty or guide me to backtrack.

Occurrence has taken place that I expected, are these mistaken imagined memories? The main difficulty I face is in me, my thoughts, nothing solid. So, I am of hope that I have just been programmed to think a certain way and none of it is true.

Respect

Do you consider all everything? Do you respect all people, all things, all of life? How about yourself? I must reiterate, I am not preaching, these are the potent lessons of my life and what knowledge, I have gained during my short research years. I am in no place, I am not one who can dictate to others because I live with regrets and failures, these have taught me. I learn the hard way, share my trials so you may learn by me. By your research you come across these words and they will forever stay with you and alter bad habits making for productive change to your persona.

I had great respect for some of the wrong things, minimal respect for a few of the right things but thought I was doing fine. Thought I was an individual with emotive talent that made me correct in most situations. I did not succumb to an opposition in opinion, whether this was advice or suggestion from friend or foe, I was right. It took rehab to identify and help me recognize the narcissist streak in me.

Do not get me wrong I was mostly content with my character but a narcissist will not even spot fatal inconsistencies, even be skilled at hiding them. Upbringing is the foundation for developing attitudes. For family and health reasons and lack in certain areas I grew with few character building rules, and made my own to fit comfortably with my developing ego.

Talk to children about their feelings, thoughts and fears, you will get more sense and effecting dogma than you may realize. A considerate deep conversation is quite possible kept to a juvenile lingo and will have profound effects on the growing childâ€™s ability to communicate and operate, it would too bring you into a real closer relationship. I have trepidations, I am talking like I know when really I do not, I am no psychologist or expert I have not even got my own kids and I am lecturing about child rearing. How can I possibly know what is best for different families? I do not, I base all I say on my experience and what I now know lacked. Which I know partly taught me the nucleus of wide uncommon knowledge or maybe I am thinking too much so, that my experience was like no other, there will be similarities that imitate to degrees and there will be those who can grasp what I say and those that say you did not see nothing you want my life!

Lives are different with included same nuances this is why I can put ideas out there. All the relationships I had lacked substance and were often fronted with facades of all kinds. You will be overwhelmed at accepting a child can often sense these and it effects their behaviour even when they do not know what the quality is or what it means, they will be determined by those invisible forces I mentioned earlier. As I said, now I have demonstrated my reasoning, all forces invisible and the like should be taken into consideration.

With the help of narrow experiences, I am half way up the

staircase.

All my writing is based on self-experienced knowledge growth, I do not claim to be nearly expert in any field and where I offer advice or ways of living, I am not preaching or insisting my advice should be listened to, it is merely a perspective that I think will assist some while go as common knowledge to others, and I do not insist it is accurate all the way, I am not organized enough to approach this as a professional piece of writing, I have not researched then written about every topic. I researched, listened to audios and lived it in a large part then I wrote remembering facts.

I do not grandeur my stories but feel they will assist those who need to learn. I have seen minority clusters of society; I have suffered to a degree. I have experienced dark recesses behind closed doors, I have been broken very broken and down, but I have also climbed from the depths. With the help of all narrow experiences in society, family life, disability, mental-health, giving talks, writing researching and more, I dominate enemies to rise and realize, I am half-way up the staircase.

Take a look at yourself, have you been sincere with your own being? I have not until I spent time away from familiar surroundings and past-times was it that I more fully accepted that I was not happy. I very quickly decided I would make some very big changes, nothing felt right so I will change everything, I chose these based on felt correctness, my feelings what felt right I assured I would alter. I feel better but anxious about promoting such change in unpredictable environments. It is how we move forward into change, dare to feel the fear. The explorer did not know what was round the corner, he only found treasure by defeating obstacles and continuing despite his trepidations and facing his fears.

Take what you can how you will, I hope you are not inclined towards pity, some people are grateful for the simplest of information, I am reaching a helping hand to those in need but still not all consider this simple info, contained herein is similar and far-reaching. Them who manage fine can still learn by witnessing realms they may never enter. You want holism? This is how to get a bit more of it.

My future is unfocused

Have murky goals and ambitions, yes I have had highs that I include in this writing when I sound definite that I have a plan but I have come against some big difficulties in my surroundings, all I shall say is they are with an essence and continue to expand, thatâ€™s enough, I claim victory.

I intend to write more, have dreams of where to get published, I want to eventually turn my writing into public-speaking. It has been a long winding road, up and down until that spark influenced my desire to self-medicate and self-improve. My rapid success foresaw another self-made mission. On the rapids I started to go against the current, climbing and saw the beginning of a phase of climbing.

I was on top, recently though I stumble and recognise at

the same time. Stumble because of my words seemingly having impact on the greater picture, temporarily I think, do not feel so much guided in this writing but I refuse to stop now. I have done a lot but I am only just getting started, my past but not much seen at other times determination is of Viking stature â€¦ was at the time of writing.

I realize just now I am guided by all those people in my past, theyâ€™re words rescheduled.

Hereâ€™s why I conclude my unfinished businessâ€¦ I wrote a pamphlet years ago, have since mislaid the last copy it never got published but that was just the warm-up, a different calibre mind was responsible. Years later much in between I start a journal, it was menial every day stuff until I changed tact, I did these two or three times, it got better and slowly was turning into a book. I scrapped the first parts, then I scrapped it all except the last few chapters. Then I made a Blog, included the last few bits wrote some more, rushed it was not at all professional or ethical and it was taken down the day after I completed and published. Was mortified but learned. Set about starting over with plans to edit the best of the Blog and pamphlet, do some more writing, get a new word editor and completely start from the outset. I start over still planning to involve the good edits but a total new direction with new overall aim is key. I need to focus and deliver much more efficiently, but the sudden lack of obvious idea generating guidance and my writing has taken on a basic, simple expression. I know this may be a good thing to keep it simple but I do not want to repeat myself or insult audiences. Also, my guidance, imagined or not, gave depth to paragraph after page. I am sure it will return; I think this is a wanted by many piece, I will continue, after all I have enough inside me right here, right now to inspire, challenge, teach and inform generations.

This writing comes so easily I assumed I was receiving guidance, there are certainly voices from my past that I can recall the meetings when ideas flourished because of this I am thinking I may publish anonymously sharing credit with these people and all guidance. Am I not giving myself any credit? I know I can write but my latest or previous latest work had depth and was the best ever in my opinion. I call on whatever and whoever to assist this to its optimal form, as I really believe it can help and change lives in its entirety. Thanks, I promise to share/give credit. Like I said it is not recognition that I want, I need this to go out to the world and have a successful enhancing impact.

Once new a man POTS OF GOLD

Once new a man, he had acquaintances but no real friends, he had relocated his life in many different areas. In all of which mystical happenings haunted him, he was scared and alone with no-one to talk over his dilemas with. He was recovering from tragic life events in his own way by his own means. He settled in a town, he thought his time had started moving again, but the socializing was drink and drug fuelled, this just suppressed his feelings of separateness. That went on for years meeting one or two people, then being manipulated by them resulting in, once he saw their true intensions, them falling out. He went back to solitude, he does not recall the exact moment but he started being alert to opportunities. Synchronicity started occurring but the drink meant it went unacted on, this continued for some time until he began recalling the meanings of these so-called coincidences. He set out encouraged by listening and following one of these occurrences and it led him to a small pot of gold at the end of the rainbow. He really put effort into listening for the hidden message and the pots of gold got bigger and more frequent and had more effect on him.

He was encouraged by an invisible force to set about searching. He had multiple health complaints mental and physical, but in one of these pots of gold he learned about self-discovery which led to self-development which in turn opened many light filled doors. He started a mission that was never completed in the past, he had an accident years before, after years of recuperating he was reborn and felt better than ever, then had it all wrenched from him at the last hurdle. So he learns, long after near defeat, he continues searching and researching his discoveries and proclaims to do some self-work, he has nothing else to do with his days. A discovery about the power of mind which he practiced lead to early promise, he saw improvements, big improvements holistically. He quit drinking, he had stopped the drugs months before, and just with just this action he rose to new heights.

He expanded his research where he mixed his knowledge of mind with acquiring knowledge about reality. He soon accepted that he had created/morphed his lifeline, all his struggles his experiences. So, he chose to morph anew, his disability dissolved to a degree, he stopped requiring drugs for his head he learned placebos and techniques and gained knowledge that was enough to keep him on an even keel, in fact some days he felt marvellous and confident. New company started appearing which developed into making good new friends. His social life grew, he still did not drink and he barely had the time he was so busy researching and writing. He thinks, he thinks he would like to educate others of this life enhancing discovery, it is early days he still wants to work on himself but for the first time in his life he has definite goals and a plan.

He discovered purpose and belief. His mindset was becoming one track minded, he could see his north star and set course to continue.

DREAM the BIG dream it comes true

I am beginning to dream again, the fact everything that is happening tells me I am not alone, means I am thinking after my epic failure, there is still chance to go on and take a similar path. It is doing things the hard way buts that is what makes character. My dream, which has changed since I started writing, I was conforming but that isn't my model of reality. That will bring me no satisfaction at all. In my dream I overcome mammoth obstacles, I make it my way, I suggest we talk about spirituality and my suggestion is heard. It is the biggest secret kept from the average man, is that a morality issue?

There is no justice, no equality in awarding the lucky few and resisting the rest. Some, the average man suffers more with struggles that are not issues in other realms, if you are considered on higher grounds you're blessed. I am starting to believe even I have powers and contact with The Higher Mind. I did anyway at one point.

I am told I am thinking from a purely human perspective, we are all spiritual residing in a... Having a human experience. Have denied me spirituality so I am going do the best I can with what I have got. Mysticism neednâ€™t follow my every move or affect me in non-human ways, though it is nice receiving guidance and inspiration and ideally, I would want it if it were backing me, the last thing I want is any kind of opposition from whatever the statures of probability are, I have witnessed all callings I mention in small degrees. Enlightenment means I would look at it from a wider angle, the bigger picture, I do not know but the texts tell you to dream big and I am questioning, only if they think I am doing wrong. My merely human brain, with a half a mind left and whatever temperance, moralities I can muster, thinks that executing an endeavour to join forces with other social-warriors to approach issues, and greatly reduce drink-driving, #each about how self-healing miracles can be done by anyone, educate the uninitiated that they need to live a moral life and reduce crime, give children a good start in life and promote the power of all of our minds to create and control life determinants and disability education is the feat of a champion, I do not want much recognition just the negative aspects of my informed future/afterlife/next life were all informed in error. It is not a catalyst for living a fatalist last life and doing, enjoying what I can in this life. Only I control my destiny so, I have changed all that. If it is right that we choose our lives before we were born, then I chose this life to experience and impact some very big subjects.

Thought my promising start in life meant it would all be ok, I would not have to try, and successes are part of the natural process of my life. My attitude was taken care of, and my naivety put to a halt and changed my view of certain destiny and an easy life. Some of the most successful, talented actors, writers, inventors and the like have no schooling and a very dramatic tough life story behind them. I needed everything that has occurred in my life to occur, to change me, make me more qualified and experience the hard times so I can talk/write better about improving and experiencing the better times. (These times were difficult but nothing compared to horrors you hear of; I have had a reasonably good life compared).

The more I dream, the more synchronizes in my days, I do not think my dreams are too much after all, I am going to keep them big and add to them, some of my goals are a lot to aim for but dreaming gets me there. I sense I am on a mystical adventure, with ethical decisions included.

I plan to do all this, and execute public speaking with no mind, that means a now smaller imagination and poorer memory, lack of confidence and more. Do it the hard way or no way. I sense there is no Divine objection, much.

It was #nferred by a third party what I was to carry out

and what not to do, but this is contained in every successful story, self-help book or career is to go with your feeling and ignore the rules if necessary.

I hear people should practice their speech thirty times; I have not even narrowed down yet I have too many subject areas in this writing. Drink driving is a big topic I tackled before and plan to include and the others, they are all large topics is general wellbeing, improving yourself, mind over matter, reality and disability. May yet hone down and focus on one or two areas but I think they all need a mention.

They say a talk using visuals goes down better, I am going to learn to be more emotive and expressive but I will at some point want to get a slide show sorted, I discovered a device which assists all this but this is distant when I'm talking at TOASTMasters or doing a TEDtalk! Aim HIGH. I will rise in confidence and practice them at lower levels before. They say that what you believe is likely to come true, no one says you have to constrain your beliefs. I BELIEVE in doing this for mutual benefit, I BELIEVE I can with preparation and practice, I BELIEVE I will do this all. As I think with good intention, expect it and believe in creating my view of the future, more occurs to help make this more likely, I discover the exact assistance I need to get there, when I am there and what I need to do today, now. I am reality making, oh wow now that has to be every-one's biggest dream! I would have thought, can you think of something else?

There is a lot of work to be done, but I am on a single track that only goes to one place, that place is my success.

Think good thoughts with me, help push my direction, do it with me and you have my word I will move mountains for a better tomorrow for us all.

I was quite negative before I started writing, got inspiration from self-healing but still uttered unpromising words, kept getting writers block, found it necessary to document my dull everyday life and all the little things and contact I had with people (have not included the dull days). Now I feel a spark has ignited, I am unstoppable, with days of doubt admittedly my strength of mind wavers but often I have a one-track mind to benefit others. I have done harm in my illusion of a past but intend to prove my worth.
Biological, transitional encapsulation.

I have done the thought impossible by even professionals and those close to me, they are proud. I stopped drinking, stopped drugs and stopped all medication. I used to have an injection to subdue mental health problems with my thoughts. I am quietly proud too; I could not see me ever managing without meds to settle me and alcohol to accompany me and pass the time. My life was a fairly quiet sorry existence.

The stories may well present slight irregularities of sequence because I will use some writing that I kept in no order that I wrote in the close past. It will be a mindful tussle back n forth in parts, all this demonstrates my mind categorization after a near-death experience. I am twenty years into recovery and making the biggest mental gains today. Rehab, research and life knowledge have all affected this. Just know that life is never ever over no matter how bad things get, this journey we all take together is my proof to you that I am right in saying this.

I said just today to someone that I had previously written, I have had a fairly quiet, easy and good life regarding comparisons of suffering. They said immediately that they did not think I have had any of these present, I agreed to a certain extent but still consider the unlucky ones. Who may well, as we all grow accustomed to familiarities, they may consider their own experience better than another even mine. We cannot compare lives, even it being helpful and settling at the right time to the right degree without it determining an outlook.

I have thought life unfair, is it, it is what you created, how you created it! I have never thought woe it is me poor me, never have I wanted to be someone else, in my temporary worst sufferings I may have had the skittish desire but it was transitional and I grew because I had had this thought that could not come true, so I thought. I am of the belief today that anything can come true. If you admire another, dream of being like them then they are an ideal role model, try to think how would they treat this event, what would they think, how would they react? And before you know it you will be growing into your ideal persona. I was a secondary nervous again at the thought of standing and giving talks in front of a crowd, so I researched, watched some talks obtained a few role models from here and other successes and I just from this noticed when I practiced a talk out loud that I was adopting characteristics and expression that I witnessed and encapsulated me so imagine really working on obtaining qualities and skills displayed by people you admire. Add real desire to your ambitions and anything is possible, you can change if you want to into whatever, whoever you desire. We are not, it was thought we are programmed at birth biologically with much even most of our inbuilt character and even our health, this is simply not true. You can build the highest sky-scraper or the widest bridge that reaches infinity. You create and build, walk on your path but let it include research, dig for golden treasures they are there.

Search around Powers of Mind, Reality, Placebos and Genetics. These are just a few to get you hooked.

Honesty and truths are powerful

Honesty and truths are powerful forces, emotionally I jointly affected someone earlier dramatically with these and some home truths. Whilst he was digesting these, his reception of the facts involved wrong thinking and reacting this led to him displaying as a psychological mess. He shall remain unidentified but he was not able or willing to look at himself and his actions in years gone by, he was trying his best, thought he had an idea what was for my better interest and could not understand why things he had learned from and/or enjoyed in his youth, I did not get the same even similar response from. Also, at another time at the end of a precarious year of rehabilitation, a woman insisted, despite my want and plea to exit, that I should stay on, because she thought it best. Because I stayed, I went on to face the most powerful truth. I was appreciative of discovering the truth but faced obscenities jointly as a result.

We cannot impose on others even with good will what was a success for us will be different for them and how is someone out of that scenario, never in it, supposed to know what is best from the other end of a phone line? We can make suggestions and guide towards our intentions and if our premise is right, the suggestion will be grabbed and followed, if wrong it will be short lived, do not take it to heart just accept that all lives need to tread vastly different paths and keep open to finding that solution. Maybe you are a parent guiding youngsters, guidance should be a sensitive accommodating mission.

I am not a parent nor am I guiding anyone, so who am I to offer advice? I realize this gentle simple advice because I spoke with this man and he admitted all I talk about, also admitted thinking you were not interested, so I suppose I gave in. I was on the receiving end of wrongly dealt with intended good deeds, I offer advice as a reciprocant, I am only too aware of the ructions and sentiments exposed. They added to and lead to 30years of resistance and stubborn opposition. Being on the receiving side of anything can make most people quickly into an expert but only to their own models of reality, and their own minds. They will broadly understand the topic in question but the detail of individualities goes unseen but should be consciously acknowledged. There are many invisible factors of different spheres of life that still need acknowledging. Do not ignore what is not solidly there, this in my experience makes for the greatest considerations and wholesome people persons. Any who desire to better themselves or reach new heights maybe are not in the elite category my hope is my time is not without reason and goes to enabling these goals.

Take a look at yourself, have you been totally honest with your own being? I have not until I spent time away from familiar surroundings and past-times was it that I more fully accepted that I was not happy. I very quickly decided I would make changes, nothing felt right so I will change much, I chose these based on felt correctness, my feelings what felt right I assured I would follow. I feel better but anxious about promoting such change in unpredictable environments. It is how we move forward into change, dare to feel the fear. The explorer did not know what was round the corner, he only found treasure by defeating obstacles and continuing despite his trepidations and facing his fears.

Take what you can how you will, I hope you are not inclined towards pity, some people are grateful for the simplest of information, I am reaching a helping hand to those in need but still not all consider this simple info, contained herein is similar and far reaching. Them who manage fine can still learn by witnessing realms they may never enter. You want holism? This is how to get a bit more of it.it.

Let me think about exactly what I want to pass on, I have my reminder but this is overall, there are many principles toward getting there.

Will not talk much more about the distant past except when I recognize examples, living in the past is thought of the same as holding grudges, is not advisable. It makes me edgy and uncomfortable even just in writing about it because it takes my mind back there, pictures start to form and a mind cannot differentiate between an imagined scene and a real scene, this is why the placebo works, your mind effects/controls your body, your mind is suggestible, no offense it is just a fact. Tell suggestible mind something in your imagination, it cannot tell the difference of realities, the sub-conscious thinks you must want it because you are thinking about it especially if you thank for naÃ¯ve petty courtesy which most polite individuals will, your subconscious will think you want that treatment. I am walking two paths here, mind will operate the body as if it were true and sub--conscious mind will create to make true, in body or the environment, minds are that potently powerful believe!

My reality holds many influencers a few of which I will touch on, your reality will be influenced by some possibly similar, some the same but many very different but they can some of these be tackled with similar efforts and strategies. All our realities differ, not one is the correct and only, there are millions and millions all sharing a common ground, I forget the terminology but these are my own words, I do not portray to know absolute or be an expert at anything but I share what I have learned from study, self-observation and watching society and life.

My time is for a Higher-purpose.

I have soul-searched and come to the conclusion, be it an end conclusion I do not think so but I for the time I decide that my time has been, is being and possibly will be for a Higher Purpose than just etching out my ego. I know they teach not to think like this and to always consider the self, do not determine your life by always thinking of others first, sometimes this is not practical. By the end of this writing, I will have clarified suspicions on my authenticity.

I have been writing some good stuff but these are just my judgments at a personal account of what I don't require refreshing in my mind. To my surprise it did not seem to have the same impact on others as it did me, I was knowingly interpreting between the lines. Needed upfront clarity so the message is clear to an unaccustomed mind. I am teaching myself tricks to assist a previously injured mind, you will find out about this later. Confusion easily strikes because I have been aiming to affect too many vastly different areas of humanity. Focus is key.

After a sleepless night and emotional day, I went for a nap

and woke with a much-felt higher perspective on the situation and my work, oh it is a wonderful feeling when equanimity strikes.

I am reminded of a saying and agree strongly with, you have everything you require inside you, right here, right now. So, I have approached this work with the conclusion I can fulfil most of it from my own knowledge and experiences. What is in my head and what I have learned will lay the ground for all to mimic if they wish, to achieve their own goals or gain similar objectives I set out and found.

All lives construct the owner, how you receive the construction and how you treat and/or react to life will categorize the magnitude and direction of a birth or death in emotive qualities and desires. How do you view the constructor? Do you witness the mystical or are you in denial? I was getting it all wrong. I settle to see clearer now the unexplained occurrence following my days, was all attempted guidance, I was on the wrong track and pushes for me to change direction were overruled by being unaware or under the influence of intoxicants, I am strait laced now nothing goes without recognition and often I see past temptations and enemies, enemies meant in the broadest sense. I am considering the smallest adultery, that fizzy drink or cigarette, up to bigger errors. Something important to add. Just always remember, be aware that there will be enemies, people or things who try and block your efforts and there will be heroes, things or people who assist you, this could be a small-scale hero, person or object, who knows what is right for you and unflinchingly guide you. But maybe, just maybe some enemies are heroâ€™s in disguise, blocking your efforts in order to keep you on the right path. Have you ever looked at obstructors like that?

Guidance it arrives in all fashions not obvious in identity but a situation that makes you backtrack and dampens your outlook, may have you walk backwards into a jewel. The light is switched on and you would not have found the light switch if you'd remained going in the current direction. I love it when something just feels right, especially when it morphs from first feeling bad to an enlightening moment onto cracking on with journeying in the most meaningful direction.

The man of lifetime effect and me passed each other in the hall last night, he could not sleep because of the events of the day being on his mind and I was up very late. We ended up both sitting in the kitchen, he made tea and started to say some things. We needed to talk because we both regretted earlier.

Yesterday and last night were landmarks that needed to happen if we are to go forward. I will stop myself since I learn that even thinking badly about a person or situation can affect that situation or person to negative degrees. Thoughts are powerful energy that can have an influence. We all play roles for each other and we add to the outcome by how we contemplate and think about the episode.

I spoke about positive growth in me because of unintentional actions, these shaped me with traits I was proud of, that would not have been so obviously or effortlessly gained another way without putting in years of self-work or meditation.

We set intentions, spoke about 30 years of impact on others, the in-between, and I am glad this discussion took place and certain it is going to change our relationship, it is already changing my attitude. I am for the first time hopeful of having a future with him in it if this carries on, because we both admitted to not having another definitive ally, we are both going to do much for each other.

The search for adulthood took over 30 years but last night and our actions spoken this morning are the most mature displays, I did not think or ever predict such clarity from me, surprized myself or reception from him, he took it to heart though I go on to in half a page time, comment about the mighty powers of truths and honesty.

He said I've always seen something in you! REPETITION is an obvious synchronicity, the same comment keeps arriving in different ways, it has been long unsaid but I am feeling something in me at the same time. Life is taking on fresh meaning and I am accepting. Uncovered a purpose years back, we are building up to my devastation and unveiling but it fits to tell you a little here. Had a lot of trials in life that toughened me up emotionally without me realising it until adulthood. Lost the plot fighting, drinking and drugs, became a consistent drink-driver. Had a crash. Long but remarkable recovery with lots to tell.

Started volunteering speaking in schools about disability.

Soon recognized I had a vital message anti-drunk-driving, expanded into colleges and other outlets, very successful should have continued but other factors reigned supreme and called a stop, I ended up in mental-health units for years, lost my purpose for years, something triggers a want to return to wellbeing with intention, do research and dig, find jewels of saviour repair myself holistically wish to share my story, a new similar bigger purpose uncovers because I can include the drink drive aspect but want to share routes to more than wellbeing, recovery, and discovery the power of mind and realities.

Will continue I set out with objectives, had interfering obstacles to navigate but have not realized my complete desires yet.

I had been emotionally hijacked.

A story not many would comprehend so no-one was or could help me now, it was up to me, I dreamed the biggest dream, signs and Synchronicities told me I was on the right path, and was becoming closer every day.

Let me tell you all something, I can see something beautiful in every person I meet but I do not know what it is. Everybody has their flair, with their own uniqueness to bring forward. We will discover how to unveil your flair and live to your best ability.

I was always destined for this place, something has been with me always even though I never acknowledged it, and people really did repeatedly say I had a certain sparkle, which disappeared when my mind was sucked out.

Unknown forces are still with me, I once thought they were not and I had failed utterly, nothing could bring life back but because of what I have been shown and because I took action on it there is light at the end of the tunnel.

We will get to objectives, starting from today is not easy as there is much distraction. Am severely editing unskilled writing it was put in scarce order so we speak of whatever came up that day, it is all build up to a fine outcome.

Had a blog taken down the day after it was set. What have I learned? It is that successful writing cannot be rushed or forced, I was copy and pasting large segments of mish mashed, unordered writing with topics that ruffled a few feathers. I learn I have to tone down and voice my opinions in a much more diplomatic way. There is ethics and morals which differ in every mind.

It is well known that writing is a very therapeutic form of therapy, it has certainly massively assisted my road toward returning to wellness, it helps clarify what I really think, it stops the brain cells from shutting down and keeps a personal articulateness, (is that a word?!) You know what I intend.

All topics have their place and time.

Realizing I have gained more than growing some wisdom on my journey, I own capacities of such that should be talked about to benefit the learning of others.

A few people, or even a lot of people consider differently on ideals and on the few or the many subjects that are morally, ethically or justifiably correct and right to talk about. We can all learn from each individual and how that teaching is held and spoken will have a great effect on its stamina for potency. I feel nearly all topics have their place and time and should be versed to the correct degree in the right manner, freedom of speech is paramount and the most educational subject may have sensitiveness but will do no justice being kept quiet.

A realization that this writing carries some resemblance to journaling, I record events that stir memories because I think there is something to be learned from it.

Had a little argument today with someone who has greatly influenced my life in many negative ways but from even these positive sentiments grew in my character. We have a long history and today was a harsh reminder of how things used to be and proved they potentially still can be if we either of us allow it. This process brought back memories of less good times when everything effected more, looking for the adult in me I decided not to reminisce sad days and sulk but to be open to his approaches to speak and reconcile, he has grown from our past as well, we spoke, there was a little resistance in me at first but when I noticed the talking had made me feel better it got me considering my whole current endeavour and position. I record the thoughts I had and the practice I made, there is not needless waffle there is something to take from all I say.

Nature is full of fears.
A life plan this was always meant to be, the Kingdom of Heaven is within.

I'm going to inspire you now:

You and I are not disparate from a flower, majestic and beautiful, do you know how majestic and beautiful you are just like a flower? But life maybe it is some people in your life, have a cruel way of tearing off the petals, ripping you in half and throwing you in the rubbish.
When I bailed out of school, had no direction or plans, didn't know what I wanted to do with my life. This is common ground for many minus the lucky minority. We could all have this luck and follow purpose if we took time to really understand how to use our minds.

Realize the possibilities.

I am going to uplift you all to realize the possibilities in this Divine life of ours. Thatâ€™s right ours, there is no me or mine, simply ours or us. We are together and can unite. I will share short stories that have guided us and given hope, you remember this story it guides you to a better place of being and doing. You need not practice tempting fate like I did, only remembered the Disabled chap who spoke to us in school when I realized I had done exactly as he warned against and was now in his feelings of trying to teach his learnt lessons so they would not have to continue and claim more victims.

You can grow now you may spread the saviour and you will create a more loving peaceful humanity because of it. No dampeners meant but Disability is paramount, it was a good teacher. Want to check yourselves? No, so Disability grabs your attention for possibly the first time.

Everything we discuss adds to the main topic which is simply a happy, successful community life. How you treat people, how you interact, what you think and say is all reflected back to you. Have a pleasant disposition and pleasant surroundings are abounded, a negative attitude will impact the #blue skies to darken, the dogs to growl, the passer-by to frown and bad luck to pronounce. As within, so without.

Careful imaginings.

Do you dream, do you day dream? Dream big nothing puts a limit on magnitude of desires. Be careful though what you imagine, this is the factor in creation of your reality.

Had me some negative visualizations they started coming true. Did my best when I learned the true nature of thought and counteracted these with dreaming and imagining and writing the sublime instead. These are more difficult; it is easier for us all to dwell on the negative but the best thought has chance of materializing too.

My life is and always has been designed by my own mind... with some colossal inferences but my childish colourful vivid imagination has evolved so far from the very bad to the supreme.

Learned because I did a lot wrong but I go on and encourage the best, this is what I should have done all the time, do not be near get this right from the start and serenity is yours. I think tis never too late to subdue your own mind, though I have made the winding path difficult I will gain more when I traverse.

We all take differing routes but the staple is the same for each, think best, act best, believe best and achieve best.

May you all have the best you can.

Dedicate my life to this cause.

My life purpose, my dedication has become to promote anti-drunk driving and disability equality, get the drunk drive fatalities down worldwide into the hundred thousand instead. if everyone on the planet viewed all my work, we would nearly abolish this epidemic.

Your choice remember, do you not remember? You would not choose this . . .Want a drink? How about another?

Mind you I have learned quite a bit, do you want to enter my school? The parallel society in your new reality, some pity, some hope, a lot of patronizing and desolateness, some advantage taking, less real respect more of ' okay darling, nice day, do you come out often? who looks after you? who does the housework and cooks?'

Although there are many who fully comprehend, it is my job to make these shine as the majority even take over completely!

Want another?

Sense is easy depending where you are stood, I went the arduous way for more satisfaction when I overcome difficulties... Do you want any satisfaction?

I know, I have the perfect answer. but no, actually you

could end anywhere.

Probably not the best suggestion but that is how simplistic all drinkers who drive when drunk is same for the drug users.

I suggest you avoid drinking and drugs and my suggestions are heard and followed.

Focus and deliver

You have everything you need within your minds. Once I had everything, I needed though I did not realize it when I could have made more use of these attributes, purpose uncovered after devastation enabled me to awaken to this. Found a pot of gold and continued searching.

This is the partly travelled journey which has multi roads in. Thought this had near completed but an end is always a beginning. Will make you reluctant and grateful, with some envy when I was climbing to the top. You will have awakenings; remember these they will save more than just your sanity.

Have a short time to deliver several of the most important lessons a life can teach. You can take what you will gain.

Learned lots from the un recognized aspects of gaining wisdom in my first twenty years did not comprehend the good and the bad, the heroes and the enemies had all taught me, until after conscious crushing, soul taking events and then shown the brightest beacons and near the highest heights.

The start of unconsciously preparing for catastrophe was naivetÃ©, ignorant behaviour, and unwariness though I thought I was fully competent and aware. If you are self-absorbed, you maybe will not even realize this, life passes your current bliss you miss all life has to offer, the time arrives that life and your mind will have had enough of you not listening to your instincts, emotions and intuition, let alone the signs and synchronicities of your day. A wakeup call is prescribed, will ya live will ya die, will ya pull through severely disabled and cognitively retarded, will ya acclimatize or will ya end your misery?

Yes, I was enjoying what I could, partying, socializing, and thinking of the opposite sex. Was a youth in my 21st year. Consider this I took the broad easy gate that only leads to a very winding road, I drank and I drove and I crashed very badly.

Jesus said enter by the narrow gate.

Wide and broad is the gate that leads to destruction and there are many who go in it. Because narrow is the gate and difficult is the way which leads to life, there are few who find it. Matthew

The winding road has continued, could not navigate effectively through the wide gate so will find the narrow gate complicated. Years of disability, social distortion and unknown realities I had to learn how to live again. Coped to some extent, that was my view others said I was not coping. Love conquers all, during this monumental challenge, I found what I did not recognize until I was many a turn down the winding road, found love. Happy days in some regard. This closed and a new door opened, went away for repair, and began the years of rehabilitation and hospital. Mental-health of sorts tried to hinder me, many years of uncertainty. My life went from ignorant bliss to devastation. Repair to decline. In the searching for answers phase that also took years, I went through struggles and difficulty, but once I found a small treasure, I allowed discovery and enrichment.

Discovered powers that were always mine I just was not aware. This is not about what these were, that is my time what worked for me may be different for you, just am facilitating similar investigation in your own life because that is a message I want you to take. Is this, learn, grow, investigate learn grow, discover learn grow. Only did two of these that came naturally, push yourself to find more because there is a wealth of unknown skill and quantities waiting. I am not here to talk about how to walk your path, I cannot possibly, only you can do that I just am advising that it is a winding road that will have many a turn but there are sign posts of different modes to assist direction and fuelling stops of different calibres to help you grow, libraries of worldly sorts to help you learn and potential everywhere you need investigate to discover. Make this part of your life plan and the rest will fall into place. I can gently guide you onto success but only you can travel your own path and achieve, mastery is waiting many levels in attainment on route. Do you investigate and discover or do you settle and plod along? Myself I was settling the signs got bigger I continued to plod on so the sign mangled my car and nearly killed me, how much more on your lap do you want. Do you think I took notice this time?

Talk of the boy and traffic lights. The three women and road, door and bureau.

Think I am taking notice now? Our experiences change our biological makeup, it is science that environment or rather our responses and reactions to that environment alter how the brain works, the chemicals it creates and the messages it sends to the body. The party lifestyle and the alcohol started the journey that led me to this truth, not a journey anyone wants to take, you will learn and grow in your reality so you do not enter a must learn new, must grow new, must investigate and discover in a socially constricted, isolating, devastating, mind warping, stigma filled reality. Your choice, it is so easy to get to that place, it is hard lived though. Stay in your reality keep your freedom of choice, take the narrow gate and get a taxi, drink driving is a choice.

Some things are in our control, some things are not.

Fortitude requires skilled temperance to adjust. Self must love, not vain in ways because this will lead to disillusion and less awareness of reality, but love for self means a love for life can be shared. Self-love will lend a confident demeanour, confidence brings about ambition which surely motivates determination, with this comes certainty in self and onto heights of inspiration.

Love all and every living thing, we are all connected sentient beings.

Once I wrote something like sacrifice nothing, this is near impossible. For gains in any area, you will have to relinquish certain traits, this is a good thing it is how change works. Make room for new gains to replace, empty the cup before you refill.

I want so research investigated to improve, help me improve other people, lessons of my life can enhance other lives without the need to mimic trials of demoralising and destruction. I have experienced triumphs that proclaimed determination but equally witnessed triumph with lack of emotive backup. Leading to a goal only half reached. Multiple factors to consider and you must take the unknown into account. My word is taken and you will unconsciously adapt to this consideration, a single person can still gain knowledge, they are not aware of every faculty and distance a person has travelled, individuality rising, guide but never ascertain.

Anti-drunk driving is the message I found purpose in the wide easy gate, but the many directions, signs and intuitions followed or dismayed created a magnitude of wealth and discovery, but and this is a butâ€¦ I chose a wrong path somewhere, and the dismay part took over and stamped authority. My path of gain when I was refilling the cup, changed because I had not emptied the cup of destructive beliefs.

This is another, when one door closes, another opens.

This is some of how life works.

Miracles and Divine intervention

This is miraculous nothing surprises me now, have to share an occurrence. Am a on certain enriched path that has been through trials partly my own life but influenced when my mind was acquired by others let's say.

Still believe a big influencer made some wrong moves throughout our season but nothing shall cause any unsurmountable obstacles, threw, over or past me shall complete. That me need to complete is made obvious to me and causes the production of masterful necessary work in a superior style.

Suggested track of music appeared as I was having a moment of despair, was entitled do not give up. Timing sublime as was myself just on the verge, Internet connection cut out immediately. Then my next view was do not give in. Absolutely amazing, listened and this surged me to continue, tried crying but been unable for years.

After acknowledging difficulties myself had some part in creating, forgetting my beneficial programming thoughts and nearly giving in, returned to work, there is still work to be done. Edited through the notes made and somehow my email was open, viewed something about podcast help, would you believe this was the exact editing necessary. A hacked podcast to stop advertising.

A new world

This will be different I am not going to mention drink driving much at the start, if you want to check stories that will definitely put you on the right path go to my blog https://drinkdrivingdeterrentslikenoother.uk but the drinking/drugs got me to this place and I absolutely guarantee with all my heart that you want to avoid this place.
A sound piece of advice for starting any project or writing I once heard is to start from where you are at.
The blog has been much based on past learning and lessons but I am in a very different place now and always did intend to talk of the future. If not my future which you

may or may not be interested in then I teach how to live your futures now and not go through what I did before you really learn.

I have created my world, every facet from my speech, thought and written word and believe I did not do this efficiently or consciously.

Because of my unplanned preparation and wavered wording I have created a world inner and outer not by choice and not in favour. Every one of us lives in their very own construction, you can construct masterfully or naively and you can enjoy or regret whatever you put into the universe through whatever style.

Creation is life, your realities will display, I am still waiting for the productive aspects I programmed which I have no doubt to develop. Just my experience is full of lessons worth sharing because everyone can learn something by me this is why I might seem to talk a lot about gone time.

I learned but was not good at putting this into practice and I once wrote that I live a life for you all to learn by so this has been accepted, I truly wish as many as possible to make use of these pages and my times.

Thought just the other day, I am not but I am, if that is decipherable I am proud to hold the small disability I am left with and my minds ability to resurrect justice for people in a similar place. Can even create equality for others but the reality I created has little of this for me I have stopped concentrating on my life and intend goodness to other people.

I am not detailing the story of my time well. Just know that you can affect your reality and that all our worlds carry influencing factors. Even these seem able to influence irregularity if not stated in the correct manner. This is a

Spiritual world. Someone suggested that to me when I was a teenager and I blissfully said I KNOW, they replied but you don't though do ya? Had no clue of all the intricacies of this fact I did not even regard them when they started to reveal. Now I fully appreciate because these occasionally are affecting in non-supportive ways.

My society and engagement with have been largely affected, firstly from my past errors in judgement and action and now to effect myself but, and I will always say this, is that there are still many, many good people about who will support my work.

I created this reality; I am not taking full responsibility. Yes, I chose to have a drink then get in a car and ended by crashing, yes, I have made some blunders first in my healthy time but just as effecting while on my path to recovery. This led to new realities in the human realm which I adjusted to and recovered from, then I was born again to discover none of this needed to present but it did because I have a purpose. Born to appreciate Spiritual worlds more fully, but I along with other influences was delicate and continued to make errors which cost my truth. Which I still say would have been acted on differently had I had an emotionally elite or even just different childhood. There are many that have had things a lot worse but I am confident in saying I do not think anyone wants my years.

Take a look at my blog I talk a little about how much family and your surroundings can influence you entire life, the decisions you make and the style in which you act as well as issues you might suffer from. I am not totally attributing this but for various reasons and people although I had a good upbringing it was all wrong. When I hear of emotionally and morally elite parents and what they teach their kids I say they are so lucky and will turnout very good people.

Spoke to someone when my mind was fully intact and had an intuition about most things which proved near very accurate, I just knew the basis of uncommon knowledge and she said some things, I replied not many people know that, she responded yeah my Dad was a Neuro psychologist. Which now I have worked alongside such for my own rehabilitation can totally grasp. There was my ego rightfully suggesting I was intelligent then I met people that have studied for their trade and skill. I was very intuitive still am but there is a haze of kinds.

People in the know surely can comprehend others people's experiences, am not talking any kind of knowing but this known can know most of the goods and negative aspects of even a quiet life, am sure I am correct so am not worried about justification any more, people know what I have been through, all details, and know that they do not want the same. There will always be those that can learn by me whether they live lives of Spiritual freedom or not, all will learn.

Orphan, explorer and warrior

Begin, orphan phase. Hold a lot of animosity because learned later in life the importance of laying the correct foundations for children. Any errors whether innocent or not, I mean if settling a child by painting a pretty setting when that is not how things are, portraying a wonderful reality when truth is you are hiding influences will do long term damage to the child's ability to engage truthfully.

middle, explorer. Search for treasures they are there. Remember growing up I thought there is more to life than this and there so is. Dreams of ambition can be realized traumas can be healed. keep exploring try new things, search in places you have ruled out

end, warrior. Just because you have gotten someplace, I am talking sentimentally/emotionally, this can even be physically, does not mean you have arrived, what will you do once you are there, how do you treat events and how will you continue to grow.

What i have learned during these.

Drinking and drugs lead to multiple places, on the chart they are all below base level of satisfactory life except a good night out but these added to heightened potentialities will affect the rest of your life or even cut this short. Driving, maybe you have a car maybe a scooter, drive your life not your vehicle. you will recall every word I say especially when you realise if you do the same thing as me and crash.

Fighting I was just a drunk boy, you are meant to be enjoying the night with friends mingling with the community not scrapping the world. this shows nothing except immaturity. none of you are immature.

Questions.

-How do you think you having a crash would affect your family? That is from my Mum, she doesn't like to emphasize but my accident had such collosol impact on everyone around me that this is the first subject she thinks of.

-Think of the benefit to not drink/drug drive, cos i am telling you, you will appreciate them after the event, and you will be cursing, these are so obvious.

-How would you feel if you were the drunk driver, and severely injured a friend but you walk away without a scratch, or even you ask a friend for lift, they end up dead or with a severe disability but again there is nothing wrong with you. This is what happened to me, a friend ask for a lift the opposite way to my home, i crashed. . . i never met him again because he felt so guilty

-Do you really know truths of the universe? If you did there is no chance you would be tempting fate and drink or drug driving or fighting or any immoral bad behaviour

-Do you really advise the best, say a family member was planning to drive after a night out would you, could you stop them or would you find it acceptable?

-Who wants regrets? Try something so prevelently taught and known by all and then live with or die from the outcome. but i suppose this is still not taught enough

-What is your learning style? Which do you like and work with best? How about oppression and imposition and by the way most choices are withheld now

-Almost like giving in when you face obstacles and difficulty, have not been the perfect model, hey if you want to try my life, all my experiences I am sure you may diverge from normality. I am trying my hardest to promote a blog, I really think and believe this can and will change worlds, is not all just one subject either, you can learn an awful lot from my times. This is a stopping intoxicated driving lesson and a living to your best course and awareness training, plus more Now this book has replaced.

I used to speak on a drink drive offender course, instead of going through the figures and alcoholic units per drink and other statistics, which are paid half attention to and little remembered I really think personal stories have a place and this is a course if gone through entirely that will totally stop anyone from even considering drink/drug driving

-I know how easily done it is, how good it is to save 20quid on a taxi, how easy the quiet at night time road is, how you are sure you will take it careful and get home. well, the alcohol makes you incapable to hold accuracy and soon you forget all this, say I was totally sober I would still have crashed! Do you remember them truths of the universe? well there was something in the road a spill or something, you cannot tell this wherever you are, whatever the time and no matter how much you have drunk. don't think you are going to get a warning either I had a few but chose to ignore them, the first time you go off the road could be enough. WELCOME to a new parallel life of disability, time to learn everything life and society and agility has to offer all over again!

This was fate unveiling, would you believe that as I was going out, I got to the town in question, it was dark and from inside a moving car, windows closed, I heard the most piercing earth-shattering clang, there was nothing there, fate was approaching, the crash happened hours later that very night!

I was destined for this place my whole life.

Again, he was insulted and hurt, the conditioning solidified when he told his Mother about the incidences, he faced every day, she simply assumed that, being less aware because he suffered brain-damage that he was mistaken and it could not have happened like he told. The boy kept quiet yielded and accepted yet another opposition.

I was that boy at the beginning, life seemed over I learned to forgive never gave up and after years of being close, after a mystical encounter I learned to live again, find purpose and have high hopes. I am now 40 and my own salvation has come about, how? Why? I have never felt alone on this voyage, a guiding light has directed discovery and intension, life is never ever over! Never, ever, ever give in!

I am going to inspire you all to realize the possibilities in this Divine life of ours. Thatâ€™s right ours, there is no me or mine, simply ours or us. We are together and can unite. I will share short stories that have guided us and given hope, you remember this story it guides you to a better place of being and doing. You need not practice tempting fate like I did, only remembered the Disabled chap who spoke to us in school when I realized I had done exactly as he warned against and was now in his feelings of trying to teach his learnt lessons so they would not have to continue and claim more victims.

It has taken you long enough, you didnâ€™t want to accept the challenge, were ready to give in, but who knows when or why but you finally welcomed the light. Realizing responsibility for a life of creating you set your mind on a seemingly unsurmountable goal. To change your prescribed Destiny!

He said Iâ€™ve always seen something in you! Repetition is an obvious synchronicity, the same comment keeps arriving in different ways, it has been long unsaid but I am feeling something in me at the same time. Life is taking on fresh meaning and I am accepting. Uncovered a purpose years back, we are building up to my devastation and unveiling but it fits to tell you a little here. Had a lot of trials in life that toughened me up emotionally without me realising it until adulthood. Lost the plot fighting, drinking and drugs, became a consistent drink-driver. Had a crash. Long but remarkable recovery with lots to tell. Started volunteering speaking in schools about disability. Soon recognized I had a vital message anti-drunk-driving, expanded into colleges and other outlets, very successful should have continued but other factors reigned supreme and called a stop, I ended up in mental-health units for years, lost my purpose for years, something triggers a want to return to wellbeing with intention, do research and dig, find jewels of saviour repair myself holistically wish to share my story, a new similar bigger purpose uncovers because I can include the drink drive aspect but want to share routes to more than wellbeing, recovery, and discovery the power of mind and realities.

Will not talk much more about the distant past except when I recognize examples, living in the past is thought of the same as holding grudges, is not advisable. It makes me edgy and uncomfortable even just in writing about it because it takes my mind back there, pictures start to form and a mind cannot differentiate between an imagined scene and a real scene, this is why the placebo works, your mind effects/controls your body, your mind is suggestible, no offense it is just a fact. Tell suggestible mind something in your imagination, it cannot tell the difference of realities, the sub-conscious thinks you must want it because you are thinking about it, I am walking two paths here, mind will operate the body as if it were true and sub â€" conscious mind will create to make true, in body or the environment, minds are that potently powerful believe!

I have a role model I desire the same success to an equal degree. I admire what he has accomplished and would like some of his achievement myself for security reasons as well as serving others, thousands and thousands of millions of other people and for feelings of self-fulfilment and usefulness. He has an admirable nature too, not at all egotist, I clarify thatâ€™s one of the qualities I evolve, humility.

The Hills and Valleys.
ABOUT and my WORTHY GOALS
Who is involved, what is their goals?
I am middle aged, had obtrusive catastrophes that taught me a lot about life, and the recovery taught me much about our true realities.
Life lessons youâ€™ll want to teach your kids.
I record a podcast on my own, on my terms, I want and try to make entertainment but its more educational. Will change things that cost billions in restoration.
The presenters voice and style is a message itself, youâ€™ll see why as the story envelops. Bare it out there are gems of wisdom contained.
Spiritual Freedom is my goal, the path is long and winding, multi levelled with many obstacles. Included are the lessons learnt from these obstacles, much research into gaining health but the main messages are of worldwide importance all with an essence, there are Spiritual lessons I have learnt all described. Drink-driving deterrents and

disability acceptance radical reduction in the figures is as I will endeavour, a mission planted. This will make all think before they drink when they have to drive home.

I am a survivor, had a drink driving car crash. Suffered the traumas of disability and society, hospitals and rehabilitation centres, a run in with a Neuro-psychologist and my own mind.

Had a wakeup and slowly but definitely restored myself after I had my mind taken.

Spiritual freedom is my goal

Who, what, when, why, how?

A survivor of turmoil wants to teach his scholar starting now, because he does not want for others to suffer this dread so he communicates his messages speaking, podcasting, blogging and by website, determined he is to change worlds.

From a brain injured survivor who learnt to train his mind and brain, heal mental-health and dissolve disability. His message will deter drink-driving and promote anti disability prejudice/discrimination. He has a dream for the world and will ensure it happens.

Made a podcast, listen and you will never drink and drive, will grow your regard and respect and general wellbeing
this needs to be in the public, I will create change.

Regards and thanks

This is highly educational and serves a great purpose, I have a dream this will be played to students, offenders and more to create dramatic changes in the world. My work is about deterring drink driving, I had a car crash under the influence. Teaching about innocent prejudices toward people with disabilities and anti-discrimination. Also mind, body and brain training, I dissolved mental health and partly a disability. Take a look, I will change societies and the world.

Thanks, regards.

From driving in the wrong lane, to conquering a self he never knew.

Visual mind.

ever knew.

Childhood was an absolute fairy tale, climbed trees and collected insects, united the whole playground to a mass game of football and won every race on sports day. Lived with Mum and Sis, though he never realized it he missed having a Father figure to teach him vital lessons of growth. Learned all his life the hard way, it continued into adulthood but he thought these lessons were meant to get easier, instead came the hardest trial to date.

He had friends to share his time with, should regard these as life was to get lonely. He had an impeccably visual mind and an astonishing imagination, could visualize anything and he did, this made him feel with might his life was profound but he figured he was nothing special and we all could do this with our minds. Later years he would discover it was no coincidence. He was to adopt the value of visualizing for healing, it is more powerful than he inclined. Did not so much require being as suitably fitting as he was, his mind would keep him company and occupy him, from an early age he did not realise but his reality was largely in the mindâ€™s eye. He too was to unfold this truth more in decadeâ€™s time.

He has heard it best not to live in the past, does not have a wealth of memories anyway, he was so caught up in his colourful mind most of life slipped by without notice, he just remembers the poor events so its best he does not transport back. Imagination can and will take you anywhere, the mind does not distinguish between a real event and a pure imagined one.

There is little to teach about being a child, except to the elders, he wishes with his shoulders that he was encouraged more to appreciation of hidden emotive, invisible qualities, independence and other foundations of adulthood. Serious conversation was replaced with little belief and expectation, he figures he would be more today if more was expected from even the kid in him. After all what a kid learns stays with them, if they learn little that stays with them, treat a kid like a child and they will mould into your desire. He did not have social parents this effects the childâ€™s growth as well.

A want to express has always laid, as a fairly non-expressive character he has though got some knowledge to share, wisdom has grown in his years, something bound after treachery. He faced a challenge and after so promising a start in life he began by not comprehending, he was certain of his destiny, how did this appear but it was not to be the worst.

He is an adult now having badly sown seeds he reaped the harvest, but eventually he recalls the Diamond seeds heâ€™d sown long ago and continues by making these prominent in thought, in mind so they will effect change.

Mind travels, Purpose uncovered.

He floated through the first part of his time oblivious to life determining dogma, he really struggled when he required wisdom but this was to grow in him.

Badly sewn seeds probably caused the reason in him to commit to searching for answers, it also led to him having to really concentrate on who he was and what he was about and this leads to purpose unveiling. He became the architect of his own identity as he was unfortunately identified by Disability after never growing up rightfully, he immaturely severely injured himself.

He had a drunk-driving car crash when 21, the entry and introduction into adulthood was mangled! Because of his limited learning and other tremendously effecting, character warping incidents or baggage this was an extra test on his durability.

He met with obstacles like heâ€™d never witnessed, the crash became obsolete and not the most determining. He learned appreciation and finally regarded his mind, he did not put to use its agility until devastation infers, use it or lose it, and he lost it! This is how he learned to appreciate, he went on a self-made mission and discovered that a vibrant mind is helpful but certainly not necessary for a happy, productive and creative life.

On he goes alongside essences and advantages, solitude and stigma, he turns all his quiet time into writing and recording. His life was not worthless helping him develop into a life educator. He began talks on Disability and anti-drunk-driving, carefully using the previous as his tool to defer, this was very successful. He once proclaimed defeat, and drank lots in consolidation but he found strength and rebuilt himself entirely through self-healing. He now wants to educate the world; he so believes his work will enhance sense and wellbeing.

Diamond seeds

He along with vivid mind dreamt dreams that create worlds! He has a vision to alter the figures for drunk drive deaths and train the people in mind, powers we all own, reality, wellbeing and healing in people who drive with stupor or hold stigmas or lack belief or want to improve themselves and their surroundings, reality making is where he is at today! He is embarking on the biggest most rewarding and worthwhile mission. This with a lost mind! He did not comprehend to satisfy the need for reward when he was too adept at dreaming so it slapped him and landed on his lap, MAKE USE OF YOURSELF!

I always did dream of having some benefit on the world but did not know how, this was meant to be, I cannot NOT change people in health promoting sense making life enhancing ways.

Focus and deliver

You have everything you need within your minds. Once I had everything, I needed though I did not realize it when I could have made more use of these attributes, purpose uncovered after devastation enabled me to awaken to this. Found a pot of gold and continued searching. This is the partly travelled journey which has multi roads in. Thought this had near completed but an end is always a beginning. Will make you reluctant and grateful, with some envy when I was climbing to the top. You will have awakenings; remember these they will save more than just your sanity.

Have a short time to deliver several of the most important lessons a life can teach. You can take what you will gain.

Learned lots from the unrecognized aspects of gaining wisdom in my first twenty years did not comprehend the good and the bad, the heroes and the enemies had all taught me, until after conscious crushing, soul taking events and then shown the brightest beacons and near the highest heights.

The start of unconsciously preparing for catastrophe was naivetÃ©, ignorant behaviour, and unwariness though I thought I was fully competent and aware. If you are self-absorbed, you maybe will not even realize this, life passes your current bliss you miss all life has to offer, the time arrives that life and your mind will have had enough of you not listening to your instincts, emotions and intuition, let alone the signs and synchronicities of your day. A wakeup call is prescribed, will ya live will ya die, will ya pull through severely disabled and cognitively retarded, will ya acclimatize or will ya end your misery?

Yeah, I was enjoying what I could, partying, socializing, and thinking of the opposite sex. Was a youth in my 21st year. Consider this I took the broad easy gate that only leads to a very winding road, I drank and I drove and I crashed very badly.

Enter by the narrow gate.

Wide and broad is the gate that leads to destruction and there are many who go in it. Because narrow is the gate and difficult is the way which leads to life, there are few who find it. Matthew

The winding road has continued, could not navigate effectively through the wide gate so will find the narrow gate very difficult. Years of disability, social distortion and unknown realities I had to learn how to live again. Coped to some extent, that was my view others said I was not coping. Love conquers all, during this monumental challenge, I found what I did not recognize until I was many a turn down the winding road, found love. Happy days in some regard. This closed and a new door opened, went away for repair, and begins the years of rehabilitation and hospitals. Mental-health of sorts tried to hinder me, many years of uncertainty. My life went from ignorant bliss to devastation. Repair to decline. In the searching for answers phase that also took years, I went through struggles and difficulty, but once I found a small treasure, I allowed discovery and enrichment.

Discovered powers that were always mine I just was not aware. This is not about what these were, that is my time what worked for me may be different for you, just am facilitating similar investigation in your own life because that is a message, I want you to take. Is this, learn, grow, investigate learn grow, discover learn grow. Only did two of these that came naturally, push yourself to find more because there is a wealth of unknown skill and quantities waiting. I am not here to talk about how to walk your path, I cannot possibly, only you can do that I just am advising that it is a winding road that will have many a turn but there are sign posts of different modes to assist direction and fuelling stops of different calibres to help you grow, libraries of worldly sorts to help you learn and potential everywhere you need investigate to discover. Make this part of your life plan and the rest will fall into place. I can gently guide you onto success but only you can travel your own path and achieve, mastery is waiting many levels in attainment on route. Do you investigate and discover or do you settle and plod along. Myself I was settling the signs got bigger I continued to plod on so the sign mangled my car and nearly killed me, how much more on your lap do you want. Do you think I took notice this time?

Talk of the boy and traffic lights. The three women and road, door and bureau.

Think I am taking notice now? Our experiences change our biological makeup, it is science that environment or rather our responses and reactions to that environment alter how the brain works, the chemicals it creates and the messages it sends to the body. The party lifestyle and the alcohol started the journey that led me to this truth, not a journey anyone wants to take, you will learn and grow in your reality so you do not enter a must learn new, must grow new, must investigate and discover in a socially constricted, isolating, devastating, mind warping, stigma filled reality. Your choice, it is so easy to get to that place, it is hard lived though. Stay in your reality keep your freedom of choice, take the narrow gate and get a taxi, drink driving is a choice.

Some things are in our control, some things are not.

Fortitude requires skilled temperance to adjust. Self must love, not vain in ways because this will lead to disillusion and less awareness of reality, but love for self means a love for life can be shared. Self-love will lend a confident demeanour, confidence brings about ambition which surely motivates determination, with this comes certainty in self and onto heights of inspiration.

Love all and every living thing, we are all connected sentient beings.

Once I wrote something like sacrifice nothing, this is near impossible. For gains in any area, you will have to relinquish certain traits, this is a good thing it is how change works. Make room for new gains to replace, empty the cup before you refill.

I want so research investigated to improve, help me improve other people, lessons of my life can enhance other lives without the need to mimic trials of demoralising and destruction. I have experienced triumphs that proclaimed determination but equally witnessed triumph with lack of emotive backup. Leading to a goal only half reached. Multiple factors to consider and you must take the unknown into account. My word is taken and you will unconsciously adapt to this consideration, a single person can still gain knowledge, they are not aware of every faculty and distance a person has travelled, individuality rising, guide but never ascertain.

Anti-drunk driving is the message I found purpose in the wide easy gate, but the many directions, signs and intuitions followed or dismayed created a magnitude of wealth and discovery, but and this is a butâ€¦ I chose a wrong path somewhere, and the dismay part took over and stamped authority. My path of gain when I was refilling the cup, changed because I had not emptied the cup of destructive beliefs, but, and this is another but, when one door closes, another opens.

This is some of how life works.

SOCIETAL RESTORATION

Received an email it said sorry we cannot promote your business.

WHAT! Itâ€™s not a business, I make no money, though would like to turn this into my career and income. I never asked to promote for my sake. Itâ€™s a societal uplift and restoration, a worldwide catastrophic epidemic I am promoting a fix for these needs sharing so the messages are heard. This is a social business, I would welcome support of any kind, look on for an inspiration.

Social business. A letter I wrote:

I am thrilled to discover your excellent business because I have a wish to start a social business that will benefit the world. To jointly effect the drink-driving epidemic and educate all on disability prejudices. 27.8million people admitted to driving under the influence and drink-driving costs the United States $132 billion a year.

Do not have anything to sell. I am educating, I am passionate about this. Am writing, also talk about powers of mind, healing and reality making.

Am condensing to shorten the message and generally brush up, is very unprofessional but I got a new microphone with better editing tools and have written so I talk more to the point.

Am not sure how we turn this into a social business. I used to give talks on some of these subjects but no longer want to travel.

Want to simply get my voice and messages out there, am good at what I do. I do want to support myself and relieve benefits.

Social Marketing sounds interesting, need help to market my product. Have an ambition to change the world I will get my podcast played in schools everywhere, this will work and put people off drink-driving as well as treat people with disabilities better without patronizing or insulting them.

REFRESHED VIEWS

Have spoken plenty about my gripes on my podcast. I am going to start having a better attitude, this is what disability can do to a lot of lives, if you acquire a disability throughout life, its very, very difficult, Society will impede, disability is a social construct not a medical model.

There are however absolute gems in this society, we can all learn from. Exposure will make a person comfortable about anything, for example when I had the accident I couldnâ€™t even say the d disabled word, but Iâ€™ve said it three times already.

I am thinking lots about a job, I am on a networking site have started to dream, I want to collaborate with people that will allow these dreams, they are big and effecting.

I am thinkingâ€¦

Heard about social businesses, to repair worldwide atrocities. I have experience in are drink-driving, thereâ€™s something like 30million deaths a year about the globe due to this epidemic. I can affect these figures, I know I can, I just need help marketing my work and my cause. The second being disability discrimination or prejudice, prejudice is not always intended but it's just as harmful.

I am trying to remain more upbeat as the last piece of work I did there was a lot of moaning about injustices. This Blog Iâ€™ll be different, that which I entertained was exactly the narrow minded albeit innocent way I used to think of disabled lives, always moaning and whinging about something. I do not want to portray that anymore. My main goal was to deter drinkers from driving, and I donâ€™t mind displaying inconsistencies as this is a deterrent itself, along with my speech and presentation. Although I learned in my writing that disability equality is an equally main goal, they both will effect masses of the world.

Heard from someone wishing to collaborate, Iâ€™m very excited, she is a creative factual writer, this fits me perfectly. Have some factual times that will come off as created but also have a story that will not seem plausible to some, I question how much of this I can release but if the essence keeps on effecting, I shall reveal all I can recall. That will make people think not only about dangerous driving but about the entirety of their lives. Think I may even want to make a film, that would be educational.

Think Iâ€™ll try my own piece of creative factual story telling:

His name is ? he always did recount the time he was told something obsolete and meaningless; they didnâ€™t stay with his conscious self for long. He never puzzled the thought that these recurring actions might mean something. Even the amazing events of his time were not considered. One day he was in the back yard on the steps listening to the birds when suddenly he had the feeling of rising up into the trees. His body hadnâ€™t moved but his line of vision was looking either into treetops or back down at himself. It was a colossal feeling that left him wonderous. They call it astral projection.

Another event years later he worked at a holiday park. He was stood on the balcony chatting with two friends, he was laughingâ€¦ Actually, he always did have this ability, his consciousness as he began to speak moved out to the side of him to observe himself talking, this gave him confidence he lacked because he could tell how he was presenting entirely. He thinks they call this observer consciousness.

The quality he was most happy with besides how he looked was his immense sense of humour, he thought a tough life had taught him but he did not really know where it came from.

Despite looking the part and having a top likeability and being good at creating laughter, he did not have the kind of luck he wished when it came to a lady. He did not have real self-esteem just a faÃ§ade of humour and maturity, he was far from real. A true narcissist will be oblivious of himself; this makes him feel today like in his younger days he certainly had a narcissism streak, which he says under his breath somewhat embarrassed but he wants to teach others and his lifetime has many a lesson.

There was nothing creative about that, these are facts!

Have had a very Spiritual life that I never appreciated, thought I was just lucky in the Genetic lottery. I was to learn a truth that would shame and I have to live with what I was reminded and what is forever with me because other people know of this too. I once thought it would be OK if people could actually hear my thoughts because behave better, more efficiently when people, when I know people are watching me. That was the narcissist talking, I talk today from an entirely manufactured altered mind, donâ€™t imagine things you wouldnâ€™t really like. Imagination is the master key to all, if you can imagine it, you can have it. Realities in my mind came to mean more than simply imagination, I have seen wild imaginingsâ€¦ Come to life, negative ones, why I was imagining them I do not know, I was a colourful shirt! So I am thinking today, that in my vigour I had some profoundly delightful, dreamlike existential thoughts and imagination was in flow, I am just still waiting for these to materialise. Thatâ€™s what keeps me going, they are the light. All I will tell you about them is to say, God has a plan for me, I shall succeed, in some way but the Law is making it more difficult every day. I will not go into that one.

Right thought we were being upbeat. What can you do?

Am intending a Blog, here it is. I overlap determinants that were, they are old news.

Was so creative in my younger day, if you are below 25, enjoy. When they said to me, enjoy, best years of your life just thought, sure, bet all adults say that. I say 25 because and only because, for the life I led, I never really grew up till then, also have said in previous writing, maybe because of my own experience but I do not think we should be OK driving at 17, think more sense in an age of 25, yeah am I alone in my thinking.

Have imagined the extreme, was foretold it will come true. I however imagine differently, and still foretell my future and my destiny, anything, anything is possible and determined thought is at the top of decision makers. Will make, am making the life I did not know until near late, but it is never to late to learn appreciation and regard.

Talk a lot about myself because I have lots to teach out of my times.

Spirituality is the biggest kept secret in the world, is that a morality issue, why does it need to be so, the enlightened few are living a very different life, of which, sure I envy, cos I was near there, but fail to see justice when I note the amount of suffering in others. I am told I am taking a purely human perspective awakening would justify.

He began very much as a follower, though never appreciated he did not know this all he thought was that he was not leader material. Was young and silly, now he has years behind him of considerable times he has substance, some knowledge of less known things he can teach others, this gives him reason and justification to hold and lead in such a position.

Know that I have value to offer and give, will create my own employment until word gets out and parties will become interested in my service, the public is my audience

I have to figure out just who will be my employer. Will serve for free to start but I want to continue in this field and refrain from relying on benefits.

Quality, quantity and spirit. Am not ready to take this out now, give me a little time, I have plans to deliver. This has become my purpose and shall derive change, wanted to proactively affect the world but will persist in delivering my lessons to the minority growing with time until hear of my work from people who do not know who I am. Spirit is the important emotive and am sure this feels right, is what I am meant to do having lost the path before. Quality is at a level I am happy with and quantity is there but have only been working with this goal for two or three days, my writing has changed and want to get a base of new material.

Personal services, appreciate the need to prepare more but want to get this public. Have enough material elsewhere but am unsure I have a solid foundation or message, though this just adds to my message without me doing any more work.

Recorded a first draft and although the perfectionist in me went back to edit to more perfection, I kind of felt good about imagining people listening, it was far from immaculate and I stubbed my toe a few times, this enhances deliverance of a vulnerable message along with what I said, have no doubt listeners will not wish to practice dangers that got me here.

Never before have I felt so much ambition certainly not with the assuredness, there is though concerns am pushing aside to continue.

Do you want a drink?

Am deciding, had clues that there is still help and that God has a plan for me. Comprehend that I will not spell out every word, I do believe have chance to make with this life something I never thought when young, did not foresee such a colloquial mission, wish I could fully get assurance of sorts.

This is phenomenal, film maker materials.

Have everything I require inside me.

Right here, right nowâ€¦

What is it I want to do?

Wish to have some beneficial effects, no matter how small scale they begin, a need to redeem my opportunity and loss. Prove myself still able to achieve great things at any level. Feel a mighty chance has flown but chances are ending, just must locate my new calling, a call of some kind is always present.

What can I do?

Can do almost anything, nothing illegal, or morally wrong, have learned the amount of aftereffect could be dealt. Can walk anywhere I wish, can eat or drink or think or say anything without any negative effects, in my reality. It is my world, my-self and my mind make the decisions that affect myself. Intend only good to happen in me and about me, and project only intended good to others, any and all harmful, negative or otherwise bad thoughts are never an intention so they are nulled and silenced. Promote goodwill to all and negate wrongful thought, my subconscious has been through many challenges itself and activity mind did not know how to respond accurate, so was affected to follow past suggestions and conditioning and I am not denying influence from my conscious self, unskilled as it was.

What did I do and what can be done about it?

Past beliefs are in the past they no longer have mercy, beliefs are strong forces but unless I consciously agree to and fully and honestly accept a belief, they have no power. They may not affect firstly me, or my surroundings. Any of civilization any territories mystical or not. Have had multiple vastly influenced thoughts and beliefs but it is only me that creates and can create anything, everything is possible so I create a repair to any and all negative in anyway bad thoughts or beliefs. Can make the future happen also can determine past influences because I believe it, I am honestly and fully accepting it is possible because absolutely anything of Mystical Spiritual essence is and always will be feasible. Reoccurring thoughts are part of the challenges I faced a bigger part I put to being placed in my once very suggestible mind, any who know the slightest of mind and sub mind will be aware that a distant forgotten memory can surface given the right conditions. This is what is happening some do not choose am remembering repressed thought/memory.

Know what me believe in, truthfully, and that suggestion can affect but will not last, not in my reality. In my reality all is perfect, a time travel back to my time of greatest wellbeing after the accident which was not all that long ago. Felt good, fabulous, walked fabulous, communicated and thought great, this time is travelling into my future to reappear alongside all added learned lessons and skills acquired thereof. Nothing absolutely not a thing is impossible in the Spiritual World we live in, and my believing Spiritual Being says I create, redeem and repair all irregularities of my true self, and take back everything that is and was rightfully mine.

What will I do now?

Thought I explained above, but justice is sometimes an awkward topic. Especially when there are rules written by many and unknown about regulations that are attached to people who cannot adhere to them or it is very difficult. Unknown laws have benefitted when was guided but where is the common ground? How do I keep these laws on my side when I am not, was not aware of the stringencies. Okay I feel I am more aware having lived through these times but there is much to remember.

A change of rule is feasible for the mighty but living on this plane with this mind it is a little incomprehensible. Fixes in my environment, the people I encounter the objects I buy and so on, were fixed to ensure my failure, yeah call me human but I find that an unfair sort of justice. Hey what is that, I am not one to talk, really, I never once asked or gave permission for my mind to be tampered with and my reality to resemble your challenges. That any person would challenge but a person recent in dramatic psychological recovery, then added to that mystical sways of identification and thinking skill, expected to complete a life altering mission with efficiency, I got close but the fixes on the path deterred direction. If this is seen through as predicted the whole scandal is immoral. I did the best I could with what I was left with. No mind oh yeah let us challenge him now.

I will be left to discover what I can develop; I will not be harmed by any, your laws cannot oppose human rules laws and regulations. You have interfered with innocent lives unsuccessfully; I can still make success I am sorry I did not complete your hopes but obviously they did not fit my model of reality. You can you think effect so much and predict the future, why did you not ensure keys lessons were taught and life prepared me. . . oh a realization, you can do all this, you did do all this. A path allowed or catered for is exactly the one I am taking. A lesson to teach many, thanks for not respecting my life, seeing a bigger purpose and use, not asking obvious questions and assuming. I am being what we humans call sarcastic, when we pretend one thing but intend another. I am not thanking anybody for taking what is rightfully mine and doing this to me unless the predictions are incorrect. I can get used to most of this but will not settle for a certain future of prediction. I want my future my afterlife my next life, to be free to live in the grace I once had.

Will continue my work, will build an empire one day, will assist my suspicions of your goals but do not expect me to backup spiritualism, you have helped destroy me, I fight back and continue good work, helpful lessons and just watch me build an empire of kinds. I am not defeated ever.

Normality maintains even flourishes on a bright day, with features that exude quality of surreal posture. Am treading carefully, need to continue.

Medication I do not require, was other factors influencing but most of these do not affect me any longer. People cannot, should not try and determine what someone does or does not do if they have no understanding of past effectors. Judgement should not be made on what one considers best if they are far from all the actualities. Talk of different factors, if a person is away from a situation how do they possibly know what is going on. Even when in close contact people do not know all, actualities in mind, make personal decisions and should be accepted. If they are foreign to your nature learn the lingo before you make judgement. All isms are missing elements of acceptance and congruity. These lead to wrongful grasping of intention and language. We should not base anything on assumption of rightful grasping.

Write because I think will enhance others and is good for me. There are lessons to be learned but I am taken for every letter misconstrued then you project. That is not the name of why I am doing this. Thought my writing was wanted. Why are you making difficulties? You want me to be honest, tell my story? How can it be done?

I am wealthy in all categories, fitness and ability, imagination and mind agility, communicating, money wise, articulate and brilliant at writing captivating pieces of work, my skin is subtle all is perfect. I am perfect I have perfect abilities in all these.

Go on to create an empire, am very successful. No longer require benefits I support myself in the future. Am free to practice what I choose to do without it affecting anything or anyone, in my creation. I have thousands, of people involved in this empire and experts running process to serve.

Have what I need, know what I need somewhere in my mind so this emerges when ever asked

Proactive productive seamless coordinate what I write becomes apparent to myself and helpful in ways noticeable leading to good. Myself the only battle I have is with thoughts, where they originated is another story, I win thought becomes easy to decipher, follow just them that produce good. My every move does not necessarily intend other action, my every thought will become chosen if not chosen they can only be ones that are helpful to me, and enable the help intention I can offer others.

My metaphorical speak of hero and enemy. My own or my own influenced thoughts are just some. You see I am in a battle to conceive a destination. I have, no they are not always an enemy but since the turning point, they have certainly made me aware of presence. Now I do not know whether these are human malfunctions or mystical, I suspect the most, they are humans with mystical qualities. Whatever but I am still not convinced if they are trying to make difficulty or guide me to backtrack.

Occurrence has taken place that I expected, are these mistaken imagined memories? The main difficulty I face is in me, my thoughts, nothing solid. So, I am of hopes that I have just been programmed to think a certain way and none of it is truth.

Sense is easy depending where you are stood, I went the arduous way for more satisfaction when I overcome difficultiesâ€¦ Do you want any satisfaction.

I suggest you avoid the drink and drugs and my suggestion is heard and followed.

Divine prosperity

Drink-driver learns the hard way.

Ready for some revealing content? My mate got a shiver listening, you all are assured to at least have a second thought when it comes to driving after intoxicants. Reveals you do not want what you can so easily have, the next chapter gets better right to the finish.

I have achieved my production.

Introduction.

Always wanted to educate others in important lessons but

underestimated myself, my life has showed me I know some vital things if you want to succeed and even live an ordinarily productive life. By ordinary I intend to teach something magnificent but maybe you are happy with just simply a plain productive life with nothing from the ordinary, have knowledge that can transmute ordinary to extra.

Thought a calm first 20 years was to continue, unemployment, study, searching unsuccessfully in the wrong places and few friends since school age. Life goes on, lost the plot at 21, no direction, drinking, fighting and driving, driving destiny and my car. Had a colossal drunk-drive car crash.

Years of recovery, acceptance and denial, life finds us meeting, will not waste your time, virtually honor a life just because this life allows me to give to you sublime teachings. They taught me, still are so there is no reason you cannot make the best better and get this knowledge upfront.

I dream today of how life would have evolved if I knew this stuff punctually.

This will help you decide.

DRINK-DRIVING, LIFE CONSEQUENCES, DISABILITY, HEALING, SELF IMPROVEMENT: Do You Really Need It? This Will Help You Decide! You had what you consider to have been a hard time over the years. You are a fool; you drank and drove. The Truth About DRINK-DRIVING, LIFE CONSEQUENCES, DISABILITY, HEALING, SELF IMPROVEMENT So you had family trouble, did you really. So you had health issues. Yes I was quite unlucky. Were they life or death situations. Well no but one of them got me emotional and they could have been life threatening. .

So you suffered losses. Yes I left many friends behind and lost all my possessionâ€™s. Were these losses equal to many other peopleâ€™s. They effected me lots I was not really considering other peoples trouble.So you think you are poised, well educated, streetwise and dignified with respect, regard and good morals. You are regaining emotive quality and brain power, you lost all once. You are still the fool, you crashed did you not.Rebuild yourself from that. Lose your dignity did you. What happened to your regard and respect. Did you find there are many in society that do not hold the same of both for you after acquiring a disability. No answer.You had enough money to go out more than once a week so why did you not put a taxi fare aside. Did you need the money that much. No answer. Did it cost you in the end. No answer. More than money. No answer. Why were you speeding, I know alcohol increases confidence but it decreases cognitive function and coordination. No answer.Want To Step Up Your DRINK DRIVING, LIFE CONSEQUENCES, DISABILITY, HEALING, SELF IMPROVEMENT? You Need To Read This FirstYou did not have much of a life in the early recovery did you. That is just one consequence. Other consequences are ability to hold a job or even get employed, you were unemployable, physically and mentally. Loss of earnings meant the need for benefits, this is a process, the first application needs proof from Doctors from occupational therapist letters and they send their own doctor to do an assessment. These are all added appointments you have to attend in your getting busy calendar, if you have no one to take you it would include public transport which is difficult with no money.You cannot balance on a moving bus either so there is trouble if there are no seats near the front, you have to stay sat until the bus has fully stopped or squeezing down the aisle on a luggage filled train especially if you are carrying anything in your good arm, before the train sets off, also it is too much of a step getting off trains.Your inability to move successfully in the environment, this as well as transport issues includes steps, curbs, uneven pavement, gravel, grass thatâ€™s more than a few inches tall, escalators and do not even think about going out when the pavements have ice on them. This leads to losing contact with mates, they were losing interest anyway, unless they are the proper sort and stay with you, you were too difficult for them and changed much from the person they knew over reacting wrongly or just thinking off-key. This is saying how difficult it is for family, they cannot just up and go if you get laree, which you probably will. Loss of independence, you cannot get anywhere without transport, you cannot be left on your own and cannot eat by yourself. Need help with the masses of forms to be filled and letters to write.You have forgotten or cannot practice the things you used to enjoy, sport, playing musical instrument, drawing or writing, socializing, driving, fishing and you cannot enjoy the thing that got you here alcohol, for some it is the sentimental reasons, others just two pints gets you drunk and off balance enough to fall over.

Do not Want To Spend This Much Time On DRINK-

DRIVING, LIFE CONSEQUENCES, DISABILITY, HEALING, SELF-IMPROVEMENT. How About You?You had plenty time before to get you into this state, drinking and driving and socializing this is the replacement in your new life. You do not get so many choices now what you do. You require benefits, Doctors, physio and other professionals so must make all the appointments, do not worry hopefully you have someone who knows you that can accompany you to explain the difficulty. You are staying in that place if you do not do your exercises, tell you what you can socialize all you like at the day center for people with disabilities. Will be different to anything you have tried before, get out and spread your wings. Rehabilitation will make you all better if we can eventually get you in but it could be a long process. Ah finally you got in it was a long year I bet but told you how much you would improve. Yes butâ€¦ They told you to continue your rehab, join a gym, attempt a sport or athletics, practice moving your affected side even eating on that side. Increase your walking distance. This is your replacement for all the fun you had in the day center, the exercises and hard work. The isolation and appointments in your newer new life. It takes how long, you join a gym but moved house and start drinking again, wasted months before you realized an opportunity. Well done you stopped drinking, improved massively and started research on self-healing. Genetics and the placebo, thought power and telling your mind and body how it behaves in the now, even if it was not true you spoke, thought, imagined and visualized your dream truth, you lived the dream for a bit did you not. It takes commitment and dedication and persistence, your early mistakes caught up did they. You never did join that meditation class did you or work on your memory. Hows your dignity after slight relapse, all the people that help you, then you wasted years until you finally started to continue work on yourself. You shocked everyone, you did something amazing you were amazing. Yes but they were some errors and the medication was wearing off, it is regaining the right levels now. You what you started drinking again. But I am producing better work everyday, I want to make this my future, all the self suggested, everything, I can make a living from these and other topics.

Powers are available to us all, what do you think about? How do you word your thought and speech? This has gotten me into a pickle, because I did not regard the magnitude of simple imagination or harsh thinking, so the choice was taken, make effort to think and speak in kind proactive words, never utter a bad thing about others or yourself. I can offer good advice because I did not follow this so I know of the consequences, just like driving dangerous I have knowledge, you quickly become an expert when seen a situation from multiple sides.

Do you dream, do you day dream? Dream big nothing puts a limit on magnitude of desires. Be careful though what you imagine, this is the factor in creation of your reality.

Had me some negative visualizations they started coming true. Did my best when I learned the true nature of thought and counteracted these with dreaming and imagining and writing the sublime instead. These are more difficult, it is easier for us all to dwell on the negative but the best thought has chance of materializing too.

My life is and always has been designed by my own mindâ€¦ with some colossal inferences but my childish colourful vivid imagination has evolved so far from the very bad to the supreme.

Learned because I did a lot wrong but I go on and encourage the best, this is what I should have done all the time, do not be near get this right from the start and serenity is yours. I think tis never too late to subdue your own mind, though I have made the winding path difficult I will gain more when I traverse.

We all take differing routes but the staple is the same for each, think best, act best, believe best and achieve best.

May you all have the best you can.

I am going to uplift you all to realize the possibilities in this Divine life of ours. Thatâ€™s right ours, there is no me or mine, simply ours or us. We are together and can unite. I will share short stories that have guided us and given hope, you remember this story it guides you to a better place of being and doing. You need not practice tempting fate like I did, only remembered the Disabled chap who spoke to us in school when I realized I had done exactly as he warned against and was now in his feelings of trying to teach his learned lessons so they would not have to continue and claim more victims.

You can grow now you may spread the saviour and you will create a more loving peaceful humanity because of it. No dampeners meant but Disability is paramount, it was a good teacher. Want to check yourselves? No, so Disability grabs your attention for possibly the first time.

Everything we discuss adds to the main topic which is

simply a happy, successful community life. How you treat people, how you interact, what you think and say is all reflected back to you. Have a pleasant disposition and pleasant surroundings are abound, a negative attitude will impact the blue skies to darken, the dogs to growl, the passer-by to frown and bad luck to pronounce. As within, so without.

You remember a time when things seemed perfect, you were free to breeze through daily living with curiosity and trust, you believed in a magical time knowing you had support in your desires, and luck was on your side. You were too young to stop and take a breath, take heed of what perfection was trying to say. Too wrapped up in your wonderful colourful mind, neednâ€™t notice the little vicissitudes but do you really know truths of the Universe? You are the hero here, have everything you need inside yourself, right here, right now.

It has taken you long enough, you didnâ€™t want to accept the challenge, were ready to give in, but who knows when or why but you finally welcomed the light. Realizing responsibility for a life of creating you set your mind on a seemingly unsurmountable goal. To change your negative prescribed Destiny and irradicate the majority of drink/drug-driving and prejudices against people with disabilities. Driving dreams of achievement are allowing.

Am here telling you that you write the rules. You create what you want, how you want it and when. Whether personal qualities in your character or artefacts to treasure, you own them, your mind is the tool for acquisition.

Never did regard your mindful ability much, certainly did

not put it to use in any fashion except toxic pleasures, use it or lose it, and you lose.

It may be taken away, great purpose was lining up and promise of magnificence on its return, but the wrong roads were trod. Deeds of only thought disgust but ghostly stand. You have a teaching masterful in disguise but question releasing it.

Nature is full of fears. A life plan this was always meant to be, the Kingdom of Heaven is within.

Iâ€™m going to inspire you now:

You and I are not very different from a flower, majestic and beautiful, do you know how majestic and beautiful you are just like a flower? But life maybe it is some people in your life, have a cruel way of ripping your petals away, then breaking you in half and throwing you in the rubbish.

When I bailed out of school, had no direction or plans, didnâ€™t know what I wanted to do with my life. This is common ground for many minus the lucky minority. We could all have this luck and follow purpose if we took time to really understand how to use our minds.

I was 17 got myself arrested spent a night in the cells, I was so ashamed I didnâ€™t dare call anyone for a lift when released, I didnâ€™t have any friends who drove, that was a time I did not have many friends at all and I certainly wasnâ€™t going to call Mum, oh yeah pick me up from the police station? So I walked 7miles home when I got to the last straight Mum drove past and saw me. She was worried where I had been and had been, informed by the police of my arrest because I was under 18. She seemed okay but had that terrible, enormous guilt making look in her eye.

There are only three emotions that are easily identifiable in my Mum thatâ€™s joy, sorrow and shame, one of these affects me more than the other two thatâ€™s shame. My Mum was a cool Mum back then, put your hands up if youâ€™ve got a cool Mum. Well add them all together and you nearly get my Mum. I didnâ€™t want her to be shameful of me.

I got up the next day, walked in the kitchen, looked at her and felt shameful, she had a new look in her eyes, one of I am going to teach you a lesson but also with a little bit of hope that her intension will have a positive impact on me. She said youâ€™re going to start work and I think you should pay some board and help with the housework while you stay here and Iâ€™m taking you to meet someone.

I agreed to the first two but insisted she tell me who were going to see, because my immediate reaction was, I donâ€™t need counselling. She did not tell me I did not know until we arrived.

We went to see Bob, he owned a wood yard and had agreed to let me start work, as a dogs body but I was happy because this man was very special because he had said something to me, he said son, I can see something in you, but I do not know what it is! I thought yeah people have said similar things before but it never reveals itself, well back to today a minute, it is revealing some more.

Bob still helped me develop into a better person, we would talk after work he would always tell me grand stories about life, culture and philosophy. I was a lost soul before working for Bob he helped me realize I can dream. I went away feeling good. So I enrolled in college to better myself, but dropped out.

Mum never gave up, she was still on a mission to get me to realize something but I did not know what. She said we are having a Halloween function at work, you can come along. Oh great I thought, she worked with Disabled, Mentally ill or otherwise very vulnerable people. Thatâ€™s going to be some partaay.

We were there, I was very uncomfortable having a drink stood at the front of a room full of seated people I could only feel sorry for, when a man sat at the back had come forward and approached me, he spoke, he said to me I can see something special in youâ€¦ but I do not know what it is. I said, yeah funny that someone said exactly that just the other day.

Repetition is how we learn but the naivety in me repeatedly ignored and forgot, synchronicity was something beyond me back then. If the time is right, I am not sure what else constitutes its occurrence. This sequence of co-incidence, being another wat to describe Synchronicity, can be phenomenal, chance like you are witnessing life talking to you. Happenings Synchronize it is so apparent that whatever the occurrence it simply cannot be ignored, you just have to work out what message is inferred. These can guide you very well to the right deed or destination.

Went back to wasting my days doing nothing but being wrapped up in my mind that I couldnâ€™t impress my friends with anymore because I did not have many. It is hard to feel majestic and beautiful when you are broken, I knew it not but I was not broken, I was just Jack without a beanstalk. I would be worse in the future but I lived for the moment and did not look or plan into the future.

They exist and I had encouraging but affectless, on my wrongfully decisive character, meaningful words from many people trying to pull me out of the rubbish. I say affectless, that is until today, when theyâ€™re words help me become whole again. Words pull together to hold meaning now where they did not before. These great people were trying to piece me back together but I have had to do a lot of that myself, okay I have people and rehab but it is when you learn to only rely on yourself totally, thatâ€™s a big milestone.

There was a trigger one day, donâ€™t know what. . . There is a lot of these unknown forces isnâ€™t there? Will talk more about them later.

For me to really quit the drugs, stop drinking, eat better, start walking more and exercising and mainly start to concentrate on myself was a clear sign I was starting to think of myself and my future more.

I had been emotionally hijacked, a story not many would comprehend so no-one was or could help me now, it was up to me, I dreamed the biggest dream, signs and Synchronicities told me I was on the right path, and was becoming closer every day.

Let me tell you all something, I can see something beautiful in every person I meet but I donâ€™t know what it is. Everybody has their flair, with their own uniqueness to bring forward. We will discover how to unveil your flair and live to your best ability.

I was always destined for this place, something has been with me always even though I never acknowledged it, and people really did repeatedly say I had a certain sparkle, which disappeared when my mind was sucked out.

Unknown forces are still with me, I once thought they were not and I had failed utterly, nothing could bring life back but because of what Iâ€™ve been shown and because I took action on it there is light at the end of the tunnel.

We will get to objectives, starting from today is not easy as there is much distraction. Am severely editing unskilled writing it was put in scarce order so we speak of whatever came up that day, it is all build up to a fine outcome.

Had a blog taken down the day after it was set. What have I learned? It is that successful writing cannot be rushed or forced, I was copy and pasting large segments of mish mashed, unordered writing with topics that ruffled a few feathers. I learn I have to tone down and voice my opinions in a much more diplomatic way. There are ethics and morals which differ in every mind.

It is well known that writing is a very therapeutic form of therapy, it has certainly massively assisted my road toward returning to wellness, it helps clarify what I really think, it stops the brain cells from shutting down and keeps a personal articulateness, (is that a word?!) You know what I intend.

Realizing I have gained more than growing some wisdom on my journey, I own capacities of such that should be talked about to benefit the learning of others.

A few people, or even a lot of people consider differently on ideals and on the few or the many subjects that are morally, ethically or justifiably correct and right to talk about. We can all learn from each individual and how that teaching is held and spoken will have a great effect on its stamina for potency. I feel nearly all topics have their place and time and should be versed to the correct degree in the right manner, freedom of speech is paramount and the most educational subject may have sensitiveness but will do no justice being kept quiet.

A realization that this writing carries some resemblance to journaling, I record events that stir past memories because

I think there is something to be learned from it.

Had a little argument today with someone who has greatly influenced my life in many negative ways but from even these positive sentiments grew in my character. We have a long history and today was a harsh reminder of how things used to be and proved they potentially still can be if we either of us allow it. This process brought back memories of less good times when everything effected more, looking for the adult in me I decided not to reminisce sad days and sulk but to be open to his approaches to speak and reconcile, he has grown from our past as well, we spoke, there was a little resistance in me at first but when I noticed the talking had made me feel better it got me considering my whole current endeavour and position. I record the thoughts I had and the practice I made, there is not needless waffle there is something to take from all I say.

I have soul-searched and come to the conclusion, be it an end conclusion I donâ€™t think so but I for the time I decide that my time has been, is being and possibly will be for a Higher Purpose than just etching out my ego. I know they teach not to think like this and to always consider the self, do not determine your life by always thinking of others first, sometimes this is not practical. By the end of this writing I will have clarified suspicions on my authenticity.

I have been writing some good stuff but these are just my judgments at a personal account of what I donâ€™t require refreshing in my mind. To my surprise it did not seem to have the same impact on others as it did me, I was knowingly interpreting between the lines. Needed upfront clarity so the message is clear to an unaccustomed mind. I am teaching myself tricks to assist a previously injured mind, you will find out about this later. Confusion easily strikes because I have been aiming to effect too many vastly different areas of humanity. Focus is key.

After a sleepless night and emotional day, I went for a nap and woke with a much felt higher perspective on the situation and my work, oh it is a wonderful feeling when equanimity strikes.

I am reminded of a saying and agree strongly with, you have everything you require inside you, right here, right now. So I have approached this work with the conclusion I can fulfil most of it from my own knowledge and experiences. What is in my head and what I have learned will lay the ground for all to mimic if they wish, to achieve their own goals or gain similar objectives I set out and found.

All lives construct the owner, how you receive the construction and how you treat and/or react to life will categorize the magnitude and direction of a birth or death in emotive qualities and desires. How do you view the constructor? Do you witness the mystical or are you in denial. I was getting it all wrong. I settle to see clearer now the unexplained occurrence following my days, was all attempted guidance, I was on the wrong track and pushes for me to change direction were overruled by being unaware or under the influence of intoxicants, I am straight laced now nothing goes without recognition and often I see past temptations and enemies, enemies meant in the broadest sense. I am considering the smallest adultery, that fizzy drink or cigarette, up to bigger errors. Something important to add. Just always remember, be aware that there will be enemies, people or things who try and block your efforts and there will be heroes, things or people who assist you, this could be a small scale hero, person or object, who knows what is right for you and unflinchingly guide you. But maybe, just maybe some enemies are heroâ€™s in disguise, blocking your efforts in order to keep you on the right path. Have you ever looked at obstructers like that?

Guidance it arrives in all fashions not obvious in identity but a situation that make you backtrack and dampens your outlook, may have you walk backwards into a jewel. The light is switched on and you wouldnâ€™t have found the light switch if youâ€™d remained going in the current direction. I love it when something just feels right, especially when it morphs from first feeling bad to an enlightening moment onto cracking on with journeying in the most meaningful direction.

The man of lifetime effect and me passed each other in the hall last night, he could not sleep because of the events of the day being on his mind and I was up very late. We ended up both sitting in the kitchen, he made tea and started to say some things. We needed to talk because we both regret earlier.

Yesterday and last night were landmarks that needed to happen if we are to go forward. I will stop myself since I learn that even thinking badly about a person or situation can effect that situation or person to negative degrees.

Thoughts are powerful energy that can have an influence. We all play roles for each other and we add to the outcome by how we contemplate and think about the episode.

I spoke about positive growth in me because of unintentional actions, these shaped me with traits I was proud of, that would not have been so obviously or effortlessly gained another way without putting in years of self-work or meditation.

We set intentions, spoke about 30 years of impact on others, the in-between, and I am glad this discussion took place and certain it is going to change our relationship, it is already changing my attitude. I am for the first time hopeful of having a future with him in it if this carries on, because we both admitted to not having another definitive ally, we are both going to do much for each other.

The search for adulthood took over 30 years but last night and our actions spoken this morning are the most mature displays, I did not think or ever predict such clarity from me, surprized myself or reception from him, he took it to heart though I go on to in half a page time, comment about the mighty powers of truths and honesty.

He said Iâ€™ve always seen something in you! REPETITION is an obvious synchronicity, the same comment keeps arriving in different ways, it has been long unsaid but I am feeling something at the same time. Life is taking on fresh meaning and I am accepting. Uncovered a purpose years back, we are building up to my devastation and unveiling but it fits to tell you a little here. Had a lot of trials in life that toughened me up emotionally without me realising it until adulthood. Lost the plot fighting, drinking and drugs, became a consistent drink-driver. Had a crash. Long but remarkable recovery with lots to tell. Started volunteering speaking in schools about disability. Soon recognized I had a vital message anti-drunk-driving, expanded into colleges and other outlets, very successful should have continued but other factors reigned supreme and called a stop, I ended up in mental-health units for years, lost my purpose for years, something triggers a want to return to wellbeing with intention, do research and dig, find jewels of saviour repair myself holistically wish to share my story, a new similar bigger purpose uncovers because I can include the drink drive aspect but want to share routes to more than wellbeing, recovery, and discovery the power of mind and realities.

But we are here today I have deteriorated a little, writing lots and unknown forces and actions of people I have in mind have affected my energy levels. So I write preaching my goodwill and my past successes but am in an environmentally constrained recess not fully practicing what I learnt and continue preaching. I am no good salesman am I read my story, it did it for me but I lose grip!

Will continue I set out with objectives, had interfering obstacles to navigate but have not realized my complete desires yet.

Truth

I have been saying we all are creators, people can interpret what anotherâ€™s inner world is like by looking at their outer world and experiences.

If a person is a seeker they shall find. Dreamers and creators create, believers in what they do and what they hope for make their future ambition a real possibility that is likely to occur.

Always I am seeking especially when I come against a problem area in life, and most often within days, sometime within hours, continued seeking reveals more than I am looking for. This works.

I create, I believe, that the future holds a place for me to teach the world vitally important lessons I have lived through. They do not appear to me as disasters now, refreshed outlook tells me these were a catalyst for allowing my knowledge to appear. Said somewhere that I did not learn many lessons of maturity as a child growing. Although I have a very loving Mother who supported me throughout good times and bad. Life, people and events, serendipity versus trauma were my education and I am making sense of all, just today and started flowing yesterday.

Will pass my knowledge to billions, globally. Overall the message of hope is, we are led on certain paths to specific directions and destinations. The destination does not mean you have arrived, what will you do there, how do you think and what are your productive actions.

Take charge of your life, command what is true and what is not., you are the Master. My time has been multi levelled and tried a decline recently by my own words as what you put into the world, you shall reap. Same for your mind, sow seeds carefully. I have sown healthy ambitious seeds, there is no law that says there is any limit of magnitude.

Old fears I had about past, strongly influenced poorly sown seeds are abolished with an inspired new mindset of turning negativity about, seeing those things as opportunity, overcoming problems to believe otherwise. Creatively visualising my desires and destiny will make for the true truth.

BELIEFS AND PURPOSE HOLISTIC FOLLOWED

Detriment began, wholistic followed, determined belief

Began life enchanted, not even middle aged and spiritually destroyed. Was this my fault. Partly but ignorance and denial allowed an added essence to influence behaviour, belief and pessimism.

Enjoyable past times were denied if to succeed. Failure was prescribed, to teach.

Was and was, I did, I sent, I proclaim. Sent a text with included negative connotations. Behold this was to come, it became fact. The only influence I had was the sending of this text, spiritual essences made it apparent. Not my sub-conscious, though this would have impacted in some way. Your subconscious hears and records all you think and say.

Had some terrible imaginings because of this text, was in decline, they HAVE NO POWER IF I SAY THEY DO NOT. Just try and come true but I researched and discovered the power we all Disability prejudice and discrimination, prepare our young properly and learn about our minds. This can change worlds. And will.

Was told negative thoughts of mine will effect, NOT IF I DO NOT BELIEVE IN THEM AND THEY WERENâ€™T INTENTIONAL. GOD HAS A PLAN

FOR ME AND IT DOES NOT INCLUDE FAILURE BEATING ME.

HELP THE WORLD EVOLVE

I have a vision.

Can you determine a societal catastrophic influence? I can, have a dream that I can easily drop the figures from 27.8million incidents a year worldwide. I want a drop of at least 1to5 million a year, no thatâ€™s only 5% reduction7or8million. No no I have witnessed the potency of what I do, will reduce statistics by ten to twenty million! NO there is no limit to magnitude remember, and desires are quite likely tomaterialize in my world, so I even help eradicate drink-driving!

This may seem extreme to you but Iâ€™ve witnessed the potency of what I do.

Raising equality has come about as an equally massive social issue. Thirdly I promote wellbeing, mind health and powers, creating and reality. These are less vital but effect the whole world. The world is my audience, need to get my voice heard. I write as well and have a vision of other companies using my work to educate and train. My reason for this is societal change globally, I started with only this goal and was intending a social business but I thought, I dream of earning my own living with my own creation of self made endeavours.

What do I do, make, unprofessional podcast write, used to public speak maybe one day I will get back to this, but currently am concentrating on reaching a bigger audience via the Web, websites and podcast and plan to individualise the categories to blogs. But need help, making more professional podcast, blogging and marketing to the globe.

I have witnessed the efficiency of very successfully displaying my own disability along with telling personal stories of societies collision with me for this simple fact.

I continued rehabilitation by discovering and implementing self-help and healing. Improved my mind and my physical gait.

Am determined in approaching companies with large audiences, but most had the impression I was promoting business. This is a social business I am promoting so my message gets heard but have discovered I can promote to other educators that want to have a name and make good changes in the world. Will put a programme together to teach others what works and how to educate in this field. Disability equality and drink drive deterrents.

I even want to create a film or documentary, need help here. Will require funding, do not know anything about this.

This is my life purpose, help me help the world.

Hope you can help in any way.

Thanks

I am going to assist the world in people's wellbeing, train about reality creation and your mind, you are creators, you have that power. Self help has brought me to health after a tragic near death experience, I will put you off drink driving forever, talk about disability discrimination and society, I found this a most effective tool to drill the message home. Been am on one journey let me tell you everything I taught myself on this path back to independence including mind power and healing, the conscious and sub conscious, thinking skills and self help,, civilization and its stigmas, you will learn something or I will eat my hat.

I make posters am happy to help businesses, charities excetera with design. If you can give this blog a mention I will make this worth your while. Used to do exactly this as voluntary work, I am a natural, very artistic I really enjoy this sort of thing. I have been contemplating how I can earn a living, design and the blog/talks/cause, there is an opening there somewhere.

Get in touch no matter what you want, or with suggestions, proposals.

Keep me busy I will keep you happy.

Your stories

Your voices heard

Here we begin an interactive experience, am interested and think this valuable to gain your opinions, stories and lessons.

Please add to my endeavour.

Mr.Pratt.

Shall start us going: One man put his car into the garage wall with his 3 and 4 year olds in the car after heâ€™d been drinking. Very scary he said, he burned his license and refuses to drive again. He still likes a drink but respect to him. Thanks for sharing. He concluded this could have ended a nastier way, this scared me to sense.

I asked him for anonymity reasons, what name shall we give you? He quickly replied, Pratt! Because I were at the time, now Iâ€™ve got my Grandkids the incident sends shivers, possible I would never have had the chance.

. But there is always a vital, he said I would never drink and drive. He does not even drive but if he did. . . Unless I had to, kids come first, if they were in trouble I would get behind the wheel if could not get a lift. This is all very well but they could be in real trouble if he picked them up then hits a tree on the way home!

Mitch.

Drunk-driving destroyed a friendship my best friendship, many, most, no ALL my friendships! Did not have any lifelong mates because of relocation but had some good mates.

Loss of identity made me a different person to who they made friends with, plus I was confused, vulnerable and easily aggravated.

Started over, had to find a different calibre of mate, which was not a bad thing. They had to be more understanding and patient.

Believe me or not but I had some of my most valuable experiences and meetings since the accident where I grew the most, although I think that is because my perceptions were so changed from living a new reality after disability inducing.

Thanks for that revealing story Mitch.

Man on bench

This was a quick chat, he was enjoying the sunshine eating his lunch. Simply outlined my purpose and history and ask him what he thought of drunk-drivers.

He said: Do ya want the honest answer, (He started by swearing) then he said people should grow up!

Replied yeah but some people especially a young generation think they are invincible so I am educating, even older generations can still drink drive. He responded this should not be about education more about using your common sense. Yes but we require some educating to enable that because unfortunately some will refrain from sense and still be misguided in treacherous pursuits. Do not entirely agree here, this is all about educating no matter your age, the next comment agrees.

Thanks for your time.

My good friend, call him Jack

Simply says just by knowing ya, witnessing and getting told stories of what you went through have made sure, I will never drink drive for sure!

You can comprehend simple education can be just exposure, no lesson just familiarization to anotherâ€™s experience, this is why speaking to audiences about my challenges of past is powerful, though am changing tact to not come over so whingey. Witnessing my life is such a powerful tool in delivery and fixing messages in the front of mind.

Thanks, I really respect his knowledge and words.

We still have a way to go

This is a story of mine something that I experienced yesterday.

Made a poster that I thought carried a strong message, they all do but this one was different somehow.

I had been awake the full night working on various things and for other reason so felt a bit groggy but I was so enthused I printed many copies and went to distribute, went in one pub, the perfect places to promote anti drink-driving. Spoke to the girl behind the bar just said have a look at this and decide if it is something you can put up.

She started, got half way, soon as she viewed mental health she said oh no, no sorry youâ€™re ok thanks anyway.

I left got to another place then parked my scooter, had the thought then walked all the way back and said it is the community you should be apologising to this is a pub do you not get drunk drivers in.

She blushed and attempted to justify her response, as it happens they cannot advertise anything unless head office says so, another girl had said. Should have replied yeah so run it by head office.

I am sure they will not be so naÃ¯ve.

If we still have people of that calibre in the world, then there is certainly drunk drivers and disability prejudice, she displayed part of this.

We still have a long way to go in resolution, the more that assist me the quicker we shall get there.

Am not whinging talking so much about disability, that was back in the day, and mainly on my Podcast.

this is on many networks. This will teach a lot. Have simply found it one of the most effective tools to use to deter others from doing the same. No one wants disability, you can all comprehend where I am coming from, I know how I used to feel when looking at a person with a disability and know most of the population feel the same way.

Put a poster I typed up on my wall years ago, I found it stashed away, I have moved home twice since then. It had just as bigger effect on me today, will discuss it now for you all to benefit from, it really is potent stuff.

We all like to stay within our comfort zones, everyone having different boundaries but you are only really living if you are placed at the edge of your zone. Life begins at the end of your comfort zone.

Is it a catastrophe when an episode comes to an end? Whatever it may be, you are sad itâ€™s OK to be missing this time however good it was but just remember, whatever has ended is always a new beginning.

Some people do not feel comfortable when life moves too

fast, they get edgy maybe even panicky but life is movement you cannot get away from this and movement is change, you saying you'd rather it stay the same?

Events create data and truths you have thoughts about these which creates an emotional experience, if any of these descriptive words change your reality will likewise change.

Thought is a lot more than just thinking, something inside of you that cannot be observed creates emotion, ideas, memories, projections, concepts, apprehensions, comprehension and desires. All of these traits fall into the category of being just thought. It is little talked about, less appreciated and small regarded but thoughts determine our lives, this is worth discussing.

Apparently, science states it the other way about, I cannot believe that, how old is this information, I thought they had made progress in brain science. Thoughts sponsor emotion, it is always the thought that comes first even if you do not feel it like that, there is always a thought of some magnitude. You do not have to overcome emotion but create them, put thought first, a fact I strongly disagree with is that you can always choose your thought. Really?

Next time I hear you moan I'll remind you, you're in one of three realities, ultimate, observed and distorted. If you are moaning you are likely in distorted.

The events of life are created by conditions and occurrence outside of you but reality is created by the same inside you, in your mind. I didn't remember that, I thought all outside started inside. Events plus data plus truths plus thoughts plus emotions plus experience equals reality, thanks for clarifying that, it should change how we behave.

Oh, now the three realities make sense, there are three truths also, actual, apparent and imagined. Gee hope Iâ€™m in an imagined distorted one!

Rearrange your thinking and you can be in a distorted reality, imagined truths will make reality distorted. This is great news, I have simply been day dreaming all these years, reality is not real, it is simply an illusion.

Oh, great stop and think but it will do little good if my thoughts are based on imagined truth, no because that creates a distorted reality and distortion is simply illusion, not true. Wahaay. Response takes time, reaction is instant. Reaction is instinctive, responses are thought about, yeah I think about imagining my truth.

One thing, raise your awareness.

I am told mind merely responds to input, really so why have we gone through the last two or three inputs, I did not think about it I just imagined.

Because the thought comes first they reckon Only I am responsible for what I do with my emotions/feelings because they are chosen.

Oh, I contemplate now, what generates the thought that creates the emotion. No well I have had thought that I will never know where they came from, I have heard that all thought has been thought before and is just floating around the ether waiting to enter.

I went through some of my earlier writing, needs work, my majestic mind which would have easily catered for masterpieces was tampered with. I have had spiritual experiences that weigh up unfair! thats right, because I was acting as a mere human, oh I wonder why! I practiced things that are perfectly acceptable for anyone to do... except me it seems. Because I was on an illprepared mystical path I approached wrong and failed and now the perfectly capable mind has influenced detereations and because these enlightened few are aware of energy I am judged.

Hey I don't like alot of what I think I don't choose or believe. If you're so enlightened why can you not comprehend my real intension and my true being? I will tell you why, because you don't know me!

Spiritual has destroyed my life but no obstacle will defeat me, I go about and can do anything human, if this is acceptable for others is acceptable for myself.

Use of powers that are not human is also unfair. I am finding strength and will not be intimidated anymore. Spirituality has no welcome place in my reality unless is going to assist a truly massive purpose and stop hindering, spirituality has no place after what is done but I have the power to resolve.

If so wanted to have influence then make this a Spiritually open world, is easy resolved along with the massesof human societal problems, easy why you make difficult then add to others difficulty is beyond me!

spiritual influence is not in line with my model of reality, I have a far more important intension than training my failures. I am going to enhance human life, until you make this a truly spiritual life you can keep out.

multi levelled

This is a multi-levelled production, I started out to decline drink driving but turns out I have much to teach from my research and times.

I have more just arrived in memory, they come like memories but are messages to your mind. This is how a lot of useful memory works.

I so called remember getting told, you will remember this, what I tell you but do not act on it, don't listen.

So here is how so-called sacred works right? You or they listen to all you say or write. Now because I only wrote it today, I have excluded them, they are excluding all these useful memories in a sense. Well memories of people telling me one thing then saying but do not listen.

So, the past few years have been mixed, so called mental health, divine messages and definite memory now I have to deal with definite memory of diffusion.

My life is going to get a lot better, amazing in fact, do I need to tell you to listen.

Think of your family, relationships and existence

Drink drivers, think of your family and what they will have to go through. Putting up with your massively cognitive redundant ways and dealing with your new ways because I am telling you that if you live, they will be new ways.
You will not adhere to these, you will have no choice, no recollection or sense. You do not think, I did not believe I would crash, have a thought for those about you, have a thought for other road users even pedestrians. I did not kill anyone thankfully but I know drinkers who have.

Don't know about any of you but I could not live with knowing that.

If you end up with disability or mental health, probably both say you live, you will have destroyed your families lives, your life, any close to you, any friendships that aren't years in the making. I don't need to go on, destruction is one word its effects are many.

I know some of you will be thinking right now that I am just a sorry chap that wants something to do, well I am but know that I can help you.

You will find, even after or during recovery, that being in the similar place you will want, need

and suddenly sense purpose. If you are lucky enough to be living a purpose or service to others do yourself a favour and do not drink or drug drive. I am saying you may regret it in the biggest way. Everyone knows you should not, everyone says or advises to not, so why is this an issue?

my intension

Always knew I would make a beneficial impact on the world; little did I know my life would contain teaching catastrophe and a then considered quiet life was offering valuable lessons every day.

Have always been artistic as well, just did not know or think much how I can make a career from this.

After the accident which you will learn from in the blog, I got into designing, first for voluntary work I made posters and designed newsletters both for community causes. Get in touch for skilful design work you want, posters/brochures etc

Much later I got into writing more, I needed an outlet so I started blogging and making webpages.

This is my offer to worlds; I shall repair epidemics.

If you diligently even scan through this page, I am sure you will be cured of multiple complaints. My life is designed for this objective.

I since recently figured to reach the most audience and potential custom need to have a place here so welcome to my webpage you are assured to achieve more than you came looking for.

Ask the universe

Was mostly content most of my life, well far from really

for multiple reason but was a camouflaged happy. Something was still missing but this remained elusive, until middle aged this was hidden partially revealing in increments.

Core beliefs, my true nature and self-have fronted unrealized goliath powers which were redirected, I am still learning and slightly opposing but the opening of a new phase is mine and I am becoming complete, am creating supreme concepts.

This is my attempted resolution to figuring out my reality.

Learned to keep exempt anything less than a good intended word, my reality is shaped by this, we all have this ability I am just working out magnitude.

Social integration is main, for various lessons I have travelled through spheres of acceptance and seclusion. Sustaining inclusion has become less easy through my own creation, so I can make that ease reappear. I am opening to and expanding my consciousness I am cultivating no less than my best brilliance.

Choose to regain full control over my thoughts, actions and speech in a truly acceptable way. I am so articulate and always have ample to say.

The way I work best is to have conversation that gives me opinions. I have vast opinion about some serious topics so try me and speak, ask questions, tell stories, give me your worries and I will resolve them but you must listen and take action.

Face this or not but the younger you are the less experience you have of cause and effect; the effects can be massively affecting.

Will show you all the way
My life has been full of unappreciated later regarded lessons.

If you want to learn and/or educate you're in a good place here, you no doubt will do both. People closest to me tell of how just by knowing me they have learned and changed and so will therefor go on to educate their children.

Drink driving, discrimination, prejudice, naivety and innocence are all tackled in a successfully learned style. I used to give talks so I know the prominence of my wording.

A woman reduced to tears on a drink drive rehabilitation programme, another one that I was introduced to and warned would not change stopped me in the street to give sincere thanks for my work and promised she would never drink drive again. She was a hardened offender cured by my work.

I believe so much in what I do have been practising this for over ten years.

purpose-and-intention

Over the years

I am 16, me and my best mate, he was the same age, were

going to the shop we had just been at the wreck, the local park where everyone used to gather, play football and socialize. I have so many good memories with a vague picture in my mind of us all interacting. My mate walked behind me, the path was narrow with cars parked immediately on the road. Suddenly our worlds froze as our young conditioned minds did not know quite what to do, a severely impaired boy was on the path scuffling toward us. We racked our brains for any socially conditioned rule as to how to behave we could. Do not stare, he will never get past with that gait, should we? Should we not? Were the thoughts, I sense my mateâ€™s uneasiness too. Staring at the hubcaps on the parked cars we hopped right out the way and waited thirty seconds for him to hobble past. Ours eyes sharpened on him as he stopped to deliver an observation. Anybody else and we would have thought they are friendly, confident and social but because he was injured in his verbalizing, stature and cognition we thought he does not know what heâ€™s doing or saying, and it is the correct thing to do to ignore all this and give him the time of day, okay I can spare two minutes but this better be quick I am very uncomfortable.

We were insultingly compassionate, thought we understood the situation perfectly and were trying to make the scenario go away, when he turned the conversation round and took massive offence. No, no we did not mean it that way, I just, well, ah. Now we were two lost boys in desperate redemption appeals, no, no we did not mean it like that.. umâ€¦ Suddenly he creased up and belted out laughing. What the, he has lost the plot were our thoughts when he settled to divulge his motivation. Now this was in a way very strong of him but there are better ways to handle a situation. He said, since I became disabled most people cannot relate to me anymore, they attempt to tip toe passed me without seeing/looking at me, like you two did and if we do communicate, they are overly sympathetic, feel sorry for me or carry stigma for disabled people, just like you both did, so I learned to play with it, and reverse the tables who is feeling awkward now? We had a half normal conversation with him but long instilled habitual patterns of behaviour meant we never dropped our guard. We really were lost now, outsmarted it did not feel good we were really put in our place. We acted out a script that was written by the majority.

Socially ingrained norms affect us more than we like to admit!

I am18: It was a sunny day, I had just been into the city with my small pay-check, I went into the first pub, on the fruit machine, lost. Second pub, on the fruit machine, lost. This cycle continued until I was out of money, did not even have enough for a bus home. I was checking my pockets for loose change, everybody in the bus shelter knew what I was hoping, I looked up and I spotted a girl sat in the middle of two others in the bus shelter. Wow she is adorable, she was gorgeous, hung round for another minute when she got up took a few steps then sat back down. Oh no, what was I thinking this is bad news, I groaned. She had a physical disability, what a narrow-minded way I used to think, when you fall for someone you do not care what differences from others they have, that is what makes things interesting, it would be a dull place if we were all the same.

I wonder how many people have reacted to me like that when I was more disabled or even now. I may have missed meeting the one because she freaked at me being disabled. I had times where I consciously witnessed people realizing I have issues, thinking I am an easy target, their face lights up then they approach me and ask for a cigarette or give me a sob story why they need some money.

The social acceptance of disability needs a lot of working on, I am doing my small part to have effect on as many people as possible to create a better atmosphere for disabled lives in a partly disabled community. I have seen discrimination and stigma from every class, it need not be this way, we are all equal we are all neighbourâ€™s living on the same planet. Put yourselves in a worse off situation, put them shoes on. Do unto others as you would have them do unto you.

I am 24. Used to scuffle and hobble my way, I would attempt to walk miles before rehab. I had started voluntary work I was walking up going through the traffic lights then over the level crossing. A multitude of scandals effect disabled people on every trip where we pass by others. On this journey two girls on the other side of the road started giggling, they found my gait very amusing, this did not affect me, and they were very young though I think in my cognitive mess I shouted angrily. Kids do not affect me anymore I find it heart-warming to see a kid laugh.

I was approaching the pelican crossing, I pass a teenager just as I reached out to press the button and wait for the green man, suddenly he came running back brushed past me and pressed the button for me. Gee I can manage I thought, then he trotted off with the proud look of being such meaningful assistance in the community. Slow to think about a more adept reaction I said thanks.

An adult woman approached on my side of the road, it

was a straight long road with plenty room to pass, she looked up saw me, panicked shook her head and immediately crossed a busy main road, then carried on down the same road, there was no turning nowhere else to go, I felt her tension as she passed with a relieved demeanour. I have had this countless times; people would rather take the added danger longer route than simply pass me. Why? Assumptions about disabled people maybe, possibly they are just being considerate and giving me room with my swaying gait, certainly doesnâ€™t feel that way.

I am 25. I went in the shopping mall, nearly fell down the escalator, I stepped forward strong foot first weak side is slower to keep up anyway I was okay. I approached the exit and saw a woman look back view me and fully open the door and wait for me holding the door open. I was about 100 meters away! She waited for Iâ€™m guessing two minutes, again I did not think so fast and did not have the will to personally attack any with my crumbled confidence and conditioning that disabled people do not talk back so again I just said thanks. This is pathetic courtesy, sorry but how would you feel experiencing all I talk about, every day? The genes in the brain change due to environmental conditions, if you are constantly put down or degraded albeit even by well-meaning folk, your brain changes its setup, and the thoughts created by all this menial action go to your sub-conscious and effect your brain, mind and body. The sub-conscious will by the discrimination put a stamp on your being thus a disabled persons personality with all its anxieties, behaviour is simply hardened and increased, this goes on to affect confidence and demeanour. The moral of the story:

Believe me or not but I have been there and observed it in others, disability is made worse and more enduring due to ill-regard, stigma even well-wishers with petty courtesy. Pull yourself together man, it will be obvious when help is required, do not go about throwing silent insults about, you are doing more damage than you will ever realize.

The boys inner self-talk is getting more and more pessimistic, he is losing faith, self-esteem and building new beliefs about how harsh people are, the griminess of the world and his uncontrollable recluse into himself, the sad picture of his once bubbly personality, the silencing of his sense of humour, he was losing his character and this even effected his home life with family that tried to understand but reasoned his deteriorating defects with the brain-injury. He had lost all his friends, they parted in his really difficult days. He was awkward company reacting to everything unsuitably, he had nowhere to go, no-one to turn to. He suddenly fully apprehended why the anti-drink-drive message is so prevalent. He never took note or responsibility it caught him in the end, he now had to resign to feeling a fool and it being his own fault, do not complain! Look at life now, now what you going to do with it?

There is strong evidence that what a person thinks and feels has more effect on the brain than the actual environment does. What a double whammy he faces, hiding from outside influences by retreating inwards does you more harm than accepting a new dimension of reality. This will change him, the body effects the mind, so disability created new thought patterns and the mind effects the body, this is proven it is how the Placebo works, mind telling body to repair or, it can do the same for decline. Not only does he need to adjust to a new body, he has the environment to toughen up to, he too has learned new beliefs so must acquaint new inner scenarios. All this is unquestionably difficult, his mind reacts in survival mode and changes in his brain neurons, connections and cells, which in turn impose on emotions, thoughts and body to name but a few which go on to dramatically alter his person and character. The boy is me, now the man, still fighting against the mighty effects in society and in mind but I am a lucky one, I am winning. So, I keep telling myself. Victory will forever remain elusive in some fields; this is why we need to start making big change happen.

What is the moral of the story? What exactly am I getting at?

How we are made and remade by forces that are largely within our control but extremely difficult for disabled people facing the great opposition of humanity. So many outer influences we tend to blame our environment. It is only how we react to that environment our inner response changes the formation of the brain which changes bodily functions. The brain doesnâ€™t distinguish between what is absolute reality and what is purely imagination. Thoughts are things, it all starts with a thought that leads to a feeling leading to action and resulting in reality shaping. Your environment will follow the feelings you have, think I am lucky, I am content, feel good and it will portray in your surroundings, with more positive encounters. Believe in a cruddy world and you will see what you believe. Hard to comprehend? I will take you on a journey, I learned to program and use my mind more efficiently, still learning but I have seen my imagination come to life, I have healed mind and body from mental-health and disability, your mind is an almighty power capable of anything. This is the story of how I learned the potency of our minds to do the miraculous and I learn the true nature of thoughts and reality. We are all connected at an energetic level.

Put simply nicer thoughts equal nicer experiences and nicer neighbours! That simple!

I can predict... or make rather

My self have created the obstacle so myself can summit the incline.

Nothing will defeat or inherit less than tremendous.

My self shall repair all worlds.

Drink driving will become a horror in history.

My self can predict.

My self can repair old history and make new such.

My self creates worlds to be all inclusive heavenly and enriched Divine.

My self has the energy to emerge anything but only super.

Myself can practice interrogations to redeem the almighty.

Justice apprehended and displayed and quantified.

Supremacy is mine to equal.

Alter ego into articulate linguistics.

What other enterprises say is free and cannot impede me.

Nothing shall decline except the negativity I antidote.

Mine views are forever upholder only the supreme.

Have grown so much, I will not lie but, even after mutual agreement from my mother. Now I must say first I had a luxurious supportive up bringing. Just for various reasons that I will keep down if you do not mind, and remember, mother agrees.

She made a pleasant atmosphere out of a potentially aggressive one. Even to the little, educational telling offs.

How was I ever going to mature on time? Due time, half my life is gone and I feel like it is just starting!

Have heard it wise to only focus on the destination and not the obstacles I want to avoid and to make small alterations for big differences on the journey and in the destination. These are good metaphors for everyone to follow if they want achievement in life.

Do not follow the crowd dare to diverge, I made my own way of delivering anti drink-drive messages and there was early success.

I am a well intending influencer hoping to access worldwide audiences with my work. So, I concentrate on achieving a great audience and influencing beneficial impact on topics I present, I start small, this will grow over time and yes, I find it difficult to know what changes to make and what idealistic future I envision but this does not mean I stop trying. Will keep on until I have more proof of the value of my work, I have gained verbal compliments, some very inspiring about the talks I have done and my written work.

Previous guided writing

Divine Prosperity, drink-driver learns the hard way.

Ready for some revealing content? My mate got a shiver listening, you all are assured to at least have a second thought when it comes to driving after intoxicants. Reveals you do not want what you can so easily have, the next chapter gets better right to the finish.
I have achieved my production.
Introduction.
Always wanted to educate others in important lessons but underestimated myself, my life has showed me I know some vital things if you want to succeed and even live an ordinarily productive life. By ordinary I intend to teach something magnificent but maybe you are happy with just simply a plain productive life with nothing from the ordinary, have knowledge that can transmute ordinary to extra.
Thought a calm first 20 years was to continue, unemployment, study, searching unsuccessfully in the wrong places and few friends since school age. Life goes on, lost the plot at 21, no direction, drinking, fighting and

driving, driving destiny and my car. Had a colossal drunk-drive car crash.

Years of recovery, acceptance and denial, life finds us meeting, will not waste your time, virtually honour a life just because this life allows me to give to you sublime teachings. They taught me, still are so there is no reason you cannot make the best better and get this knowledge upfront.

I dream today of how life would have evolved if I knew this stuff punctually.

Your real world will become surreal, people even family will not regard what you face every day, just always remember, this is making you stronger even if you felt broken at first or still.

Have faith that life is going exactly as it is meant to. Coming from witnessing the Angelic to opposition I can say I want to help, know I can but the direction is imposed. I can and am trying, have a Blog, Podcasts, website and slideshow all describing what my denials lead to and an appreciation for obeying mighty powers and again what denial leads to.

Suggested topics I am somewhat skilled in after learning the hard way:

-Teach children to be grown-ups. Mature conversation is quite possible but more importantly teach morals, dignity and absolute no noâ€™s.

-Do your own research on life realities, connection of all and thoughts and intention. -Drink-driving is an absolute no no, youâ€™ll regret it when you find that place in my past!

-Disability equality, all of us have differing appearance and ability, in the broadest sense, it seems the wider the differing gap the more unaccepted and a forced punishment on carrying on equally in society is pushed upon.

-Divine experiences, the light has shined my whole life but I only noticed when this was loudest. I grow in respect and admiration. . . Or is that jealousy? The capacity dreamed of became reality but my stubbornness spoiled one path, so I made another but because I deferred a little before I repaired the indiscernible everything was making difficulty.

We are all Gods of our reality.

Because I wrote I overcome any obstacle and I take the tough winding route for more satisfaction when I get to the destination it has been tough.

A quote, sorry cannot recall where from ..just because we have reached the destination does not mean we have got there and completed our journey. It goes roughly.

This is an all-inclusive venture, send suggestions for topics of debate and support.

-Another one I have experience of is self-improvement and self-healing, mentally, emotionally and physically. Belief and faith played a big role here, these are two most powerful words.

Drink-driving is the preferred UK term for driving under the influence of alcohol. The US equivalent is drunk driving, driving under the influence (DUI) and driving while intoxicated (DWI). Statistics (UK) 10% of all accidents with injury are caused by excess alcohol; 33% (66% if between 10 pm and 4 am on Friday and Saturday nights) of all drivers and motorcyclists killed have blood alcohol levels over the legal limit. At double the legal limit, the risk of crashing is 20 times greater than that of a sober driver.

What do we think of drivers who are drunk? There is growing disregard is there not?

Find yourself in situations I have been in and you cannot refuse it was your own doing. Lost friendships because of lost identity, awkwardness, inappropriate reactions, disability, mental health. Court, fines, bans, prison even death is not enough of a deterrent, we have to teach with upfront honest words.

Used to educate talking in schools and colleges about the drink and driving and one lucky survivor consequence called disability. I hope to get back to the public talking, this is my continued venture to educate worlds.

Disability there is no amenable word is there? Infirmity, disablement, impairment, defect, disorder, affliction, handicap, disability. I strongly disagree with the current word, you do not dis-the-able and you certainly do not dis the afflicted.

I invented a phrase years ago.. Missability, because of how most of society think it politically correct not to even make eye contact. Do not stare.. They cannot help a glimpse at your feet though as you stagger or a quick shifty up and down glance.

Or they jump back ten feet a flap their arms in giving you right of way, drawing attention is most unwanted.

Drink and drugs, like I said I wish this to be an inclusive sect, we will draw worthy sentiment from the drug user as well as the parent to the poorly child and the Divinely inspired, all are welcome, do not judge me even if you have foresight and I will not judge you.

But my child is adrunk-driving easily done, hard livedbut my child is a good person. Learn the easy way! Live and let live before it is too late. Refuse drink and drug driving.. or you can continue your learning and readjusting in a ruptured existence. Which is your favoured learning style?? Good person.

Talk of consequences, fines, bans, maybe prison, do not often include a-coma, brain-damage, hospitals for years, disability and mental-health, loss of identity, loss of friends and connections with family.

Or even, maybe you would prefer death!

Rebuild your persona from this!!

My life purpose, my dedication has become to promote anti- drunk driving and disability equality, get the drunk drive fatalities down from tens of millions worldwide into the hundred thousand instead. if everyone on the planet viewed all my work, we would nearly abolish this epidemic.

Your choice remember, do you not remember? You would not choose this!. . .Want a drink? How about another?

Mind you I have learned quite a bit, do you want to enter my school? The parallel society in your new reality, some pity, some hope, a lot of patronizing and desolateness, some advantage taking, less real respect more of â€˜ okay darling, nice day, do you come out often? Who looks after you? who does the housework and cooks?â€™

Although there are many who fully comprehend, it is my job to make these shine as the majority even take over completely!

Want another?

Sense is easy depending where you are stood, I went the arduous way for more satisfaction when I overcome difficultiesâ€¦ Do you want any satisfaction?

I know, I have the perfect answer. . . but no, actually you could end anywhere.

Probably not the best suggestion but that is how simplistic all drinkers who drive after a drink are thinking same for the drug users.

I suggest you avoid the drink and drugs and my suggestion is heard and followed.

Sense is not a mountain but you can climb.
Began life.
Lacking substance life skills education. Full of ignorance and self-importance. Was a dreamer but not dreams of goal ambitions, success and love, just kid like daydreams. Something kept telling me every things going to be ok, this was the Divine talking, which I also did not regard, higher-power guiding my thought.
Feel like I am finding that path where things are good after travelling many journeys up many paths. With many losses and continued opposition, I am strong enough to overcome. Do not doubt yourself or believe in fanciful horror stories.
I am adept at this advice for one main reason, you live through an experience and you can become proficient even expert.
Lived life.
In disregard, little gratitude and no beliefs just kept asking with my mighty mind why am I so lucky to get all this, somethings got to come of this, but I did not know what. Failed to grow up in my prior reality, so was forced to in a

beginning twisted one. Reached Divinity and through my words warped my reality again now have to rebuild my amazing path and will continue to reach the enlightening experiences of this sacred planet. Careful how and what you speak, think and imagine, only do these in good ways that enable your best to emerge and it will.

Find myself here, drunk-driving nearly killed me but since gave me the most rewarding experiences. Talking to large audiences as a person who considered himself a bit intimidated, making a definite difference in the attitudes of others for the best. Witnessing children learning, not only witnessing but creating that masterful learning environment for all. I am trying to lead others in my success so they can produce the same and finally if not totally, in the majority eradicate dangerous drunk/drug-driving and promote disability equality. We can do this. All.

Discern at right ways to live, drive, thrive and stay alive or earn the hardest learn. This slide show will educate and add reluctance to drink-driving. Educators, trainers, professionals, parents or anybody wanting to show this slideshow even to adults in denial, it will make the difference. I plan to start an industry to help drink-driving offenders or friends or family that have been affected in any way, who want to promote and teach the anti-drink-drive message. Any people who have resulting disabilities are especially successful, they have the added powerful message delivered visually or perhaps you have suffered losses because of a drink-driver.

Take this from a survivor who has learned the hard way, I

have included just some of the toils faced by being stopped by police or by being caught out entirely. Welcome to your new existence, I was caught out. I had a trauma of my own making years ago by drink driving. Now no one wants my time over these years. I have had an inner calling to stop the drink-driving epidemic, am willing to try anything, I feel a great sense of duty, I have tried public speaking, websites, blogs, podcasts, slideshows, message boards but have yet to acquire my proper audience. I want to beneficially repair worlds. My idea is to reach more people so in turn they could educate others through my hard learned lessons or maybe giving people the tools to forward the concept by simply giving a well written slideshow or you can make use of all my materials, this along with your own story will make you as accessible as I have been through, telly, newspapers and radio. About 7.1 million people with ages ranging from 12â€"20 (18.8 of this age group are 16 years old) reported drinking alcohol in the past month. The figures show that around one in 20 of all reported crashes in 2018 involved a drunk driver. The total number of people injured or killed in drink-drive crashes was 8,600 in 2017, down from 9,040 during the previous year.

How to give an effective presentation. Have a conversation, ask questions, tell stories.-Start from before an accident, when the person in question started drinking then driving. -I cannot tell how much my family was affected, I was unconscious and had a brain-damaged recovery but stories my Mum tells are very prominent and touching, so if you are talking of a family member this still can be tremendously impactful. Maybe you are a friend of the one in question, possibly there were a group in the car.-Be honest about how your disability or losses has affected your life, I find my experiences from the early days after the accident and before I started my recovery to hold power or maybe it is your acceptance or grief to be most powerful. Do not be frightened to use shock tactics, this is not hard considering the different plights we all face.-Experiences of interaction with or a lack of acceptance from, society especially resonate.

-Attempt to put the audience in the person/family in questions place, even say â€˜put them shoes onâ€™ or â€˜put yourself in such a situation. Or make use of what you can and add your own reality, we all have differing stories that will provoke sense. -Get to the crowdâ€™s emotions and you will save lives.-Make use of news, statistics and quotes. There are some easily found stats on my blog but you might want to do your own research, web browsing or things you have heard.-Be expressive raising and lowering tone and pausing at vital moments to give time for them to really digest and contemplate.-Recommend utilising the slideshow, I have had comments from adults and it made a shift in their thinking so it specially shall a younger group. I used to talk in schools and colleges and found my strategies of deliverance highly effective, I have even made adults cringe and cry on a drink-drive rehabilitation course. I stopped a mate from re-entertaining his driver license and driving again. He likes a drink.

Want a drinkâ€¦ We get taxi. HALLELUJAH

-Divine experiences, the light has shined my whole life but I only noticed when this was loudest. I grow in respect and admiration. . . Or is that jealousy? The capacity dreamt of became reality but my stubbornness spoiled one path, so I made another but because I spoiled a little before I repaired the indiscernible everything was making difficulty. We are all Gods of our own reality.

A quote, sorry cannot recall where from ..just because we have reached the destination does not mean we have got there and completed our journey. It goes roughly.

Or they jump back ten feet a flap their arms in giving you right of way, drawing attention is most unwanted.

But my child is a drunk-driving easy done, hard lived but my child is a good person. Learn the easy way! Live and let live before it is too late. Refuse drink and drug driving.. or you can continue your learning and readjusting in a ruptured existence. Which is your favoured learning style?? Good person.

Your choice remember, do you not remember? You would not choose this!. . .Want a drink? How about another?

Please email comments and feedback

You want to learn how to self-invigorate best. Do not dwell on the past, learn from this and live in the moment. Do not anticipate the future, make your dream in the now moment. Can offer worthy advice because you will learn from my mistakes. I will talk of gone days because there is much to learn from them and I am teaching others, those who listen will do good those who do not have another path to follow. Respect and appreciation, for life and for every living thing, this will come back to you and you will instantly gain regard because of what you demonstrate. Perseverance and determination, the second attributes offered as life enhancing skill the first being belief in yourself and faith in everything. Equality and justice, we are all brothers and sisters connected at unwitnessed levels, you can do good through the minimal. Differences in the same deserve equal. Belief, believe in everything, anything is possible and you can achieve whatever you believe. Belief in the Sacred is not necessary for this to lead but question things, you shall receive answers. Look for chance co-incidences, what are they trying to tell you? Life speaks to you every day, is your task to notice and take heed. Service and purpose, are the only words I would offer if you wanted the best advice on how to live a more than satisfactory, productive and benevolent life. You are the pearl go shine and share your love and light.

I am going to uplift you all to realize the possibilities in this Divine life of ours. Thatâ€™s right ours, there is no me or mine, simply ours or us. We are together and can unite. I will share short stories that have guided us and given hope, you remember this story it guides you to a better place of being and doing. You need not practice tempting fate like I did, only remembered the Disabled chap who spoke to us in school when I realized I had done exactly as he warned against and was now in his feelings of trying to teach his learned lessons so they would not have to continue and claim more victims.

You can grow now you may spread the saviour and you will create a more loving peaceful humanity because of it. No dampeners meant but Disability is paramount, it was a good teacher. Want to check yourselves? No, so Disability grabs your attention for possibly the first time.

Everything we discuss adds to the main topic which is simply a happy, successful community life. How you treat people, how you interact, what you think and say is all reflected back to you. Have pleasant disposition and pleasant surroundings are abound, a negative attitude will impact the blue skies to darken, the dogs to growl, the passer-by to frown and bad luck to pronounce. As within, so without.

You remember a time when things seemed perfect, you were free to breeze through daily living with curiosity and trust, you believed in a magical time knowing you had support in your desires, and luck was on your side. You were too young to stop and take a breath, take heed of what perfection was trying to say. Too wrapped up in your wonderful colourful mind, neednâ€™t notice the little vicissitudes but do you really know truths of the Universe? You are the hero here, have everything you need inside yourself, right here, right now.

It has taken you long enough, you didnâ€™t want to accept the challenge, were ready to give in, but who knows when or why but you finally welcomed the light. Realizing responsibility for a life of creating you set your mind on a seemingly unsurmountable goal. To change your negative prescribed Destiny and irradicate the majority of drink/drug-driving and prejudices against people with disabilities. Driving dreams of achievement are allowing.

Am here telling you that you write the rules. You create what you want, how you want it and when. Whether personal qualities in your character or artefacts to treasure, you own them, your mind is the tool for acquisition.

Never did regard your mindful ability much, certainly did not put it to use in any fashion except toxic pleasures, use it or lose it, and you lose.

It may be taken away, great purpose was lining up and promise of magnificence on its return, but the wrong roads were trod. Deeds of only thought disgust but ghostly stand. You have a teaching masterful in disguise but question releasing it.

Nature is full of fears. A life plan this was always meant to be, the Kingdom of Heaven is within.

When I bailed out of school, had no direction or plans, didnâ€™t know what I wanted to do with my life. This is common ground for many minus the lucky minority. We could all have this luck and follow purpose if we took time to really understand how to use our minds.

I was 17 got myself arrested spent a night in the cells, I was so ashamed I didnâ€™t dare call anyone for a lift home when released, I didnâ€™t have any friends who drove, that was a time I did not have many friends at all and I certainly wasnâ€™t going to call Mum, oh yeah pick me up from the police station? So I walked 7miles home when I got to the last straight Mum drove past and saw me. She was worried where I had been and had been, informed by the police of my arrest because I was under 18. She seemed okay but had that terrible, enormous guilt making look in her eye.

There are only three emotions that are easily identifiable in my Mum thatâ€™s joy, sorrow and shame, one of these affects me more than the other two thatâ€™s shame. My Mum was a cool Mum back then, put your hands up if youâ€™ve got a cool Mum. Well add them all together and you nearly get my Mum. I didnâ€™t want her to be shameful of me.

I got up the next day, walked in the kitchen, looked at her

and felt shameful, she had a new look in her eyes, one of I am going to teach you a lesson but also with a little bit of hope that her intension will have a positive impact on me. She said youâ€™re going to start work and I think you should pay some board and help with the housework while you stay here and Iâ€™m taking you to meet someone.

I agreed to the first two but insisted she tell me who were going to see, because my immediate reaction was, I donâ€™t need counselling. She did not tell me I did not know until we arrived.

We went to see Bob, he owned a wood yard and had agreed to let me start work, as a dog's body but I was happy because this man was very special because he had said something to me, he said son, I can see something in you, but I do not know what it is! I thought yeah people have said similar things before but it never reveals itself, well back to today a minute, it is revealing some more.

Bob still helped me develop into a better person, we would talk after work he would always tell me grand stories about life, culture and philosophy. I was a lost soul before working for Bob he helped me realize I can dream. I went away feeling good. So, I enrolled in college to better myself, but dropped out.

Mum never gave in, she was still on a mission to get me to realize something but I did not know what. She said we are having a Halloween function at work, you can come along.

Oh, great I thought, she worked with Disabled, Mentally ill or otherwise very vulnerable people. Thatâ€™s going to be some partaay.

We were there, I was very uncomfortable having a drink stood at the front of a room full of seated people I could only feel sorry for, when a man sat at the back had come forward and approached me, he spoke, he said to me I can see something special in youâ€¦ but I do not know what it is. I said, yeah funny that someone said exactly that just the other day.

Repetition is how we learn but the naivety in me repeatedly ignored and forgot, synchronicity was something beyond me back then. If the time is right, I am not sure what else constitutes its occurrence. This sequence of co-incidence, being another way to describe Synchronicity, can be phenomenal, chance like you are witnessing life talking to you. Happenings Synchronize it is so apparent that whatever the occurrence it simply cannot be ignored, you just have to work out what message is inferred. These can guide you very well to the right deed or destination.

Went back to wasting my days doing nothing but being wrapped up in my mind that I couldnâ€™t impress my friends with anymore because I did not have many. It is hard to feel majestic and beautiful when you are broken, I knew it not but I was not broken, I was just Jack without a beanstalk. I would be worse in the future but I lived for the moment and did not look or plan into the future.

They exist and I had encouraging but affectless, on my wrongfully decisive character, meaningful words from many people trying to pull me out of the rubbish. I say affectless, that is until today, when theyâ€™re words help me become whole again. Words pull together to hold meaning now where they did not before. These great people were trying to piece me back together but I have had to do a lot of that myself, okay I have people and rehab but it is when you learn to only rely on yourself totally, thatâ€™s a big milestone.

There was a trigger one day, donâ€™t know what. . . There is a lot of these unknown forces isnâ€™t there? Will talk more about them later.

For me to really quit the drugs, stop drinking, eat better, start walking more and exercising and mainly start to concentrate on myself was a clear sign I was starting to think of myself and my future more.

I had been emotionally hijacked, a story not many would comprehend so no-one was or could help me now, it was up to me, I dreamed the biggest dream, signs and Synchronicities told me I was on the right path, and was becoming closer every day.

Let me tell you all something, I can see something beautiful in every person I meet but I donâ€™t know what it is. Everybody has their flair, with their own uniqueness to bring forward. We will discover how to unveil your flair and live to your best ability.

I was always destined for this place, something has been with me always even though I never acknowledged it, and people really did repeatedly say I had a certain sparkle, which disappeared when my mind was apprehended.

Unknown forces are still with me, I once thought they were not and I had failed utterly, nothing could bring life back but because of what Iâ€™ve been shown and because I took action on it there is light at the end of the tunnel.

We will get to objectives, starting from today is not easy as there is much distraction. Am severely editing unskilled writing it was put in scarce order so we speak of whatever came up that day, it is all build up to a fine outcome.

Had a blog taken down the day after it was set. What have I learned? It is that successful writing cannot be rushed or forced, I was copy and pasting large segments of mish mashed, unordered writing with topics that ruffled a few feathers. I learn I have to tone down and voice my opinions in a much more diplomatic way. There are ethics and morals which differ in every mind.

It is well known that writing is a very therapeutic form of

therapy, it has certainly massively assisted my road toward returning to wellness, it helps clarify what I really think, it stops the brain cells from shutting down and keeps a personal articulacy.

Realizing I have gained more than growing some wisdom on my journey, I own capacities of such that should be talked about to benefit the learning of others.

A few people, or even a lot of people consider differently on ideals and on the few or the many subjects that are morally, ethically or justifiably correct and right to talk about. We can all learn from each individual and how that teaching is held and spoken will have a great effect on its stamina for potency. I feel nearly all topics have their place and time and should be versed to the correct degree in the right manner, freedom of speech is paramount and the most educational subject may have sensitiveness but will do no justice being kept quiet.

A realization that this writing carries some resemblance to journaling, I record events that stir past memories because I think there is something to be learned from it.

Had a little argument today with someone who has greatly influenced my life in many negative ways but from even these positive sentiments grew in my character. We have a long history and today was a harsh reminder of how things used to be and proved they potentially still can be if we either of us allow it. This process brought back memories of less good times when everything effected more, looking for the adult in me I decided not to reminisce sad days and sulk but to be open to his approaches to speak and reconcile, he has grown from our past as well, we spoke, there was a little resistance in me at first but when I noticed the talking had made me feel better it got me considering my whole current endeavour and position. I record the thoughts I had and the practice I made, there is not needless waffle there is something to take from all I say.

I have soul-searched and come to the conclusion, be it an end conclusion I donâ€™t think so but I for the time I decide that my time has been, is being and possibly will be for a Higher Purpose than just etching out my ego. I know they teach not to think like this and to always consider the self, do not determine your life by always thinking of others first, sometimes this is not practical. By the end of this writing I will have clarified suspicions on my authenticity.

I have been writing some good stuff but these are just my judgments at a personal account of what I donâ€™t require refreshing in my mind. To my surprise it did not seem to have the same impact on others as it did me, I was knowingly interpreting between the lines. Needed upfront clarity so the message is clear to an unaccustomed mind. I am teaching myself tricks to assist a previously injured mind, you will find out about this later. Confusion easily strikes because I have been aiming to affect too many vastly different areas of humanity. Focus is key.

After a sleepless night and emotional day, I went for a nap and woke with a much-felt higher perspective on the situation and my work, oh it is a wonderful feeling when equanimity strikes.

A Blueprint of desire for my promising future, starting today, my life is filled with protective encouraging light.

I involve: This event will be interesting, relevant and inspiring. I would love listeners to go out and extend what you learn to your friends, family, inner circle and whoever you can, spread the news of what I do, plant the seed.

I think I desire to duplicate one of my role models successes. As well as serving others, thousands and millions of other people and for feelings of self-fulfilment and usefulness. He has an admirable nature too, not at all egotist, I clarify thatâ€™s one of the qualities I evolve, humility.

I clear any obstacles to me attaining a fraction of his successes, I project that I dream, I magnetize a wealth of physical, material, moral and cognitive kinds. I am inspired to reach new vistas, I grow my talents and gifts and I am inspired with new ideas, I rise and I contact my higher self for inspiration and guidance and support. I improve my mind and I heal myself of all affliction and barriers, I believe in myself and my future, I give to the many important teachings, I recall all of them, I lead the public and I illumine them to a sensible route in the right direction for a contented safer life. I create a masterful presentation which I think about lots and give speeches that I am paid handsomely for. I am so happy and content that I elevate people to have a higher perspective in life, and on the universe and its invisible forces. I transmute any past conditioning they have learned and I banish all negative beliefs they hold about themselves, others, the true meaning of nature and thought form, I remove even a fraction of the biggest most harmful effecting stigmas, prejudices and discriminations, I affect large establishments with my work I even dissolve negative views in the public eye, I promote healthy changes to Education, I subdue my ego when I devise a small plan which is heard by MPâ€™s and I solve difficulties of mass suffering or minority defects.

I maintain a stable and balanced community, I influence all of society in beneficial, productive life enhancing ways. I block any interferences, and I appraise any assistance. I study hard a lot of the time and I think with this goal in sight, I comprehend more people can know just some of what I have learned throughout my life as well as during my studies, to develop and maintain a heavenly existence. I thrive on how I imagine I am received; I inspire and in turn am inspired myself, I radiate goodwill for all as I beautify the unknown as I educate, I strengthen every moral quality I possess and likewise enhance these attributes in others.

I project my feelings into the world and it is reflected back to me in society and my reality, I rectify while I remove any past negative deeds, I played any part of. I co-operate with only good intentions now which I derive much from, that I enjoy which I accredit with esteem and praise. I concentrate on where I sense great can be made, I motivate at the right times in the right places with the correct audience who can truly learn most and act on teachings, to go on and become a tutor in their own areas and promote these lessons to an even wider group.

I contact higher consciousness and I retain all I think and am guided in my learning and presenting, I discount the unimportant and un-educational and I recall the big lessons that have the most impact. I confront my fears and I negate them; I devise a plan of action, I originate most of the materials and I anticipate guidance in thinking, finding the rest and giving a well-prepared talk and being well received I anticipate all this.

I contemplate and consider my life as being worthy of character and abundance. I am wealthy, wealthy, wealthy, emotionally, morally, cognitively and physically. I write my riches to assisting charities and promoting what is I think a tremendous business opportunity, I discover suitable places for outlet, I perfect every detail and nuance and I invent my dream destiny where all past negative implications are released, I share only joy, satisfaction and excitement at a life turned around, I am proud I made use of myself eventually.

I tap the universal supply for inspiring suggestions, possible methods of beginning on a small scale and inspired idea generating for what to include in my presenting and writing. Other feasible, no matter how unsurmountable they seem, career routes I could apprehend, this may not be the one its just that which I assume at the moment that utilizes my experiences and knowledge, other subjects will show themselves soon. I accumulate mental riches early in the build up, I grow my intellect and my confidence soughs, I grow my memory bank, I increase my Emotional-Intelligence, I produce much dignity, become more assertive and gain respect so people really listen, hear me and take action I think

I contact the Universal-Mind which helps in completing a thorough Mind-Map as the one I have is in the early days of development and requires more detail and planning. I write better than ever and I stun at the quality of what I produce with the gratefully received assistance of higher minds including my higher self. Brain-waves flow and masterpiece after masterpiece are born, I think my work shall remain steadfast. Money starts coming to me from unexpected sources, this helps me in my preparation for good big things to come. I think about and use money wisely, I buy what I require with a big excess for extras, I have plenty arriving I possess a bank balance of one hundred thousand pounds. I buy whatever I choose to and I purchase for or help others in their endeavours. Going forward I share the news that we are all powerful enough to create the good life, what pitfalls to avoid in creating, we can all do the same. I am alert and in full control of my faculties and my blessed destiny.

I create, create and create, I rejuvenate my soul, I conquer my downfalls, I believe, believe and believe, will you follow me?

All my writing is based on self-experienced knowledge growth, I do not claim to be nearly expert in any field and where I offer advice or ways of living, I am not preaching or insisting my advice should be listened to, it is merely a perspective that I think will assist some while go as common knowledge to others, and I do not insist it is accurate all the way, I am not organized enough to approach this as a professional piece of writing, I have not researched then written about every topic. I researched, listened to audios and read and lived it in a large part then I wrote remembering facts.

I do not grandeur my stories but feel they will assist those who need to learn. I have seen minority clusters of society; I have suffered to a degree. I have experienced dark recesses behind closed doors, I have been broken very broken and down, but I have also climbed from the depths. With the help of all narrow experiences in society, family life, disability, mental-health, giving talks, writing researching and more, I dominate enemies to rise and realize, I am half-way up the staircase.

Occurrence has taken place that I expected, are these mistaken imagined memories? The main difficulty I face is in me, my thoughts, nothing solid. So I am of hopes that I have just been programmed to think a certain way and none of it is truth.

Talk to children about their feelings, thoughts and fears, you will get more sense and effecting dogma than you may realize. A considerate deep conversation is quite possible kept to a juvenile lingo and will have profound effects on the growing childâ€™s ability to communicate and operate, it would too bring you into a real closer relationship. I have trepidations, I am talking like I know when really I do not, I am no psychologist or expert I have not even got my own kids and I am lecturing about child rearing. How can I possibly know what is best for different families? I do not, I base all I say on my experience and what I now know lacked. Which I know partly taught me the nucleus of wide uncommon knowledge or maybe I am thinking too much so, that my experience was like no other, there will be similarities that imitate to degrees and there will be those who can grasp what I say and those that say you did not see nothing you want my life.

Lives are different with included same nuances this is why I can put ideas out there. All the relationships I had lacked substance and were often fronted with facades of all kinds. You will be overwhelmed at accepting a child can often sense these and it effects their behaviour even when they do not know what the quality is or what it means, they will be determined by those invisible forces I mentioned earlier. As I said, now I have demonstrated my reasoning, all forces invisible and the like should be taken into consideration.

Adolescents hold much innocent confusion and need just as much support in developed ways, we need to mature our teaching as the child matures. New realms of life become of interest. The one that springs to mind that I had an unrealized total lack of respect for in my teens was for the opposite sex. This resulted in behaviours of later matured realized regrets and disrespect for self, I am just glad it did not lead to early parenthoodâ€¦ or did this?

Messages of vital importance can be delivered in suitable ways even before adolescence. Children of the most emotionally elite parents display an understanding of the stakes and virtues of this high respect for all things, I kid you not. Starting off life with little or even a lot of life skills education means nothing if the holistic childâ€™s time is not catered for. A demise in one area can be enough to outweigh the efforts put into less important areas. So we must realize the Higher-Archie of development.

Early adulthood I was still a teen at heart because my brain and character had not been given the chance to produce the main virtues, only small irrelevant ones considering the cycle of life I was on. Plodded on unconsciously incompetent at living, it all passed me by, things/relationships started deteriorating, destruction was and always had been on the cards, it caught me in the end I had a near fatal drink-drive car crash. The new chapter, the new life started here.

Adulthood I canâ€™t talk much about regular lives because disability was my introduction to the search for adulthood. I learned very much about first home alone, society, past-times, friends, enemyâ€™s and heroes and how family life changes. I had to adjust an already unskilled and ill-prepared self in the adult life to new vistas and unspoken of horizons. They would change me, in part for the first part I was conditioned socially and environmentally into fitting everyone elseâ€™s far from truth realities about people with disabilities, I tried to fit into a non-obliging community. Then came the rehab incident and mental-health. The next few years, over ten of them were hospitals and units interspersed with solitary living with my own thoughts and opinions of others. It destroyed me just as severely as the crash. I lived in disbelief at the courtesy displayed and the yet newer new venture. I lived in toil alcohol dependency and drugs mist for years. One day I was enlightened to the infinite possibilities of the human mind and reality not being how it seemed. I chose to follow this hunch, I very much liked the sound of it. I conclude we are at today, I stopped the alcohol, drugs. I am no longer dependent on strong mind altering meds. I work at and climb in agilities. I focus my blank mind and after book losses or wrongful writing and a Blog being removed, a website getting hacked I start over and this has more promise than before efforts. My mind is just occasionally halfway up the staircase! I redeem defeats I announce desires and I battle a poorly made, struggle filled, hyper vigilant self that no one believed in. I am your model of creation, create life and create recovery. Create life and create destiny. Create wins along the path overcome defeat and win at your life.

EDIT: I do not feel like a recommended model these days.

Ego

Can you tell my egoâ€™s taking lead, I have studied ego much but currently recall little to inform. This is turning into simply a personal story of triumph. I did not prepare or organize or record well all the methods I discovered and used for my success. So will mention just the most promising: Visualization, things materialize, adeptness, agility, even visualize how you want your reality to look, powers of mind, truths of reality will make it so. All I can say is you have to walk your own path, what was right for me will not always fit with you. Take a look at alternative healing, new discoveries even Spiritual practices can greatly effect non-Spirituals. And do your research, look into the infinite power of mind, mind over matter, reality making and personal development. Be who and how you wish, vastly improve physically, health wise and mentally. Take no one word for gospel. Even Drâ€™s, Psychologists and professionals I have proved wrong. I lose count at how many times I refused advice and I created my ideals, follow your own rules do not go with the crowd.

My computer had wealth after masses of information on, I kept being reminded to but it seemed the wrong thing so I never did a backup. The computer shut down the other day. I still have some information, I have written lots of notes and I have my writing saved so not all is lost. I was not much phased because I am of the belief now that I have everything I need inside me, right here, right now. With memories that stir and guidance I will still make it worth your time, I will still inspire even if I do not educate or advise but I am sure you will still find all of these present, because I have lived lives of minorities and experienced miracles. I am aware that I am often too hard on myself, reading these word I conclude they are educational in some little taught subjects, I have not gone in much or broadened much knowledge but just by being aware there are things out there and I have given you a few ideas of where to start your enquiry. This will take you far.

Disability was the effect, drunk-driving was the cause. Disability can categorize as a very large topic that has phenomenal inferences when it comes to societal respect and personal major influences on ego. Do not think of ego as a power trip, most people use the word in a wrong context, we need our egos to survive.

The small rewards for doing a good deed or buying new clothes or new car, simply eating releases a reward and these all bolster ego in people, it feels good that is all, it does not mean they get big headed. A personâ€™s ego will feel rewarded for the smallest action that encourages release of a brain chemical. I do not recall which one, I should know but I am no Neuro-scientist and have memory issues certainly with these big words. I think it is Serotonin.

So you understand we need our egos for survival, have you ever, you must have, felt an ego dampener? (Again there is a scientific phrase but these are my ways). You most definitely have felt the mood destroying, confidence flattening effects of a crushed ego. Times that by many, many muchness and that is what certain disabilities induce every day. It is not just the disability it is the environment and societal responses in that immutable environment. The respect I talked of earlier vanishes, ego is not just tarnished it is utterly demolished to personality mind deviating constructions. Why do you think some/many people with certain disabilities display very similar character traits? Yes they are due in part to their complaint but the overwhelming conditioning is largely responsible, remember I have lived it. I have acknowledged changing in majority ways because of this conditioning. This happens much, a lot unseen, unappreciated and un-tackled by many.

I am realizing a new goal, it feels right, my intended mission is not solely drunk-driving deterrents, yeah I can use and have found it punchy to carefully use disability as a deterrent in itself but there is someone else coming along. I will also include the largely unspoken of disability epidemic. Just not convinced of my ability to deliver, I have my impactful short stories but thatâ€™s all really I know of society and disability I am not medically trained, yes I think I can make it a personal account broadening where possible, this will be apt I am sure. I hear a lot of voices chattering as they read my words what epidemic?? People, most people do not even see there is an issue, a lot of people able folk do not even realize. Only a person in this category will fully agree and have witnessed the issue I am referring to as effecting themselves.

A few short examples of simplistic ways societal pressures are harmful to disabled people, even the good deeds and well-wishers, if you cannot get your head round that let me describe for you, I will paint a not so pretty picture:
Disability is actually hampered, even made worse by our inner reactions. It is not the environment changing us on its own it is our responses to it. He has had a good life so far but this seemed like an end. New horizons with jagged edges and murky skies, solitude and some pity, some tolerance, some discrimination, they all will alter who he thinks he is.

I want to talk about disability, I successfully used this method to deter drink-driving in my talks, that is partly the aim here but equally I use this space to inform ignorance. My aim in this writing is to improve lives and I having been in that place wish to improve lives for people with disabilities and also the stigma creating individuals who mean no harm they just donâ€™t know any better.

I am 16, me and my best mate, he was the same age, were going to the shop we had just been at the wreck, the local park where everyone used to gather, play football and socialize. I have so many good memories with a vague picture in my mind of us all interacting. My mate walked behind me, the path was narrow with cars parked immediately on the road. Suddenly our worlds froze as our young conditioned minds did not know quite what to do, a severely impaired boy was on the path scuffling toward us. We racked our brains for any socially conditioned rule as to how to behave we could. Do not stare, he will never get past with that gait, should we? Should we not? Were the thoughts, I sense my mateâ€™s uneasiness too. Staring at the hubcaps on the parked cars we hopped right out the way and waited thirty seconds for him to hobble past. Our eyes sharpened on him as he stopped to deliver an observation. Anybody else and we would have thought they are friendly, confident and social but because he was injured in his verbalizing, stature and cognition we thought he does not know what heâ€™s doing or saying, and it is the correct thing to do to ignore all this and give him the time of day, okay I can spare two minutes but this better be quick I am very uncomfortable.

We were insultingly compassionate, thought we understood the situation perfectly and were trying to make the scenario go away, when he turned the conversation round and took massive offence. No, no we did not mean it that way, I just, well, ah. Now we were two lost boys in desperate redemption appeals, no, no we did not mean it like that.. I umâ€¦ Suddenly he creased up and belted out laughing. What the, he has lost the plot were our thoughts when he settled to divulge his motivation. Now this was in a way very strong of him but there are better ways to handle a situation. He said, since I became disabled most people cannot relate to me anymore, they attempt to tip toe passed me without seeing/looking at me, like you two did and if we do communicate they are overly sympathetic, feel sorry for me or carry stigma for disabled people, just like you both did, so I learned to play with it, and reverse the tables who is feeling awkward now? We had a half normal conversation with him but long instilled habitual patterns of behaviour meant we never dropped our guard. We really were lost now, outsmarted it did not feel good we were really put in our place. We acted out a script that was written by the majority.

Socially ingrained norms affect us more than we like to admit!

I am 18: It was a sunny day, I had just been into the city with my small pay-check, I went into the first pub, on the fruit machine, lost. Second pub, on the gambler again, lost. This cycle continued until I was out of money, did not even have enough for a bus home. I was checking my pockets for loose change, everybody in the bus shelter knew what I was hoping, I looked up and I spotted a girl sat in the middle of two others in the bus shelter. Wow she is adorable, she was gorgeous, hung round for another minute when she got up took a few steps then sat back down. Oh no, what was I thinking this is bad news, I groaned. She had a physical disability, what a narrow minded way I used to think, when you fall for someone you do not care what differences from others they have, that is what makes things interesting, it would be a dull place if we were all the same.

I wonder how many people have reacted to me like that when I was more disabled or even now. I may have missed meeting the one because she freaked at me being disabled. I had times where I consciously witnessed people realizing I have issues, thinking I am an easy target, their face lights up then they approach me and ask for a cigarette or give me a sob story why they need some money.

The social acceptance of disability needs a lot of working on, I am doing my small part to have effect on as many people as possible to create a better atmosphere for disabled lives in a partly disabled community. I have seen discrimination and stigma from every class, it need not be this way, we are all equal we are all neighbour's living on the same planet. Put yourselves in a worse off situation, put them shoes on. Do unto others as you would have them do unto you.

I am 24. Used to scuffle and hobble my way, I would attempt to walk miles before rehab. I had started voluntary work I was walking up going through the traffic lights then over the level crossing. A multitude of scandals effect disabled people on every trip where we pass by others. On this journey two girls on the other side of the road started giggling, they found my gait very amusing, this did not affect me, they were very young though I think in my cognitive mess I shouted angrily. Kids do not affect me anymore I find it heart-warming to see a kid laugh.

I was approaching the pelican crossing, I pass a teenager just as I reached out to press the button and wait for the green man, suddenly he came running back brushed past me just to press the button for me. Gee I can manage I thought, then he trotted off with the proud look of being such meaningful assistance in the community. Slow to think about a more adept reaction I said thanks.

An adult women approached on my side of the road, it was a straight long road with plenty room to pass, she looked up saw me, panicked shook her head and immediately crossed a busy main road, then carried on down the same road, there was no turning nowhere else to go, I felt her tension as she passed with a relieved demeanour. I have had this countless times, people would rather take the added danger longer route than simply pass me. Why? Assumptions about disabled people maybe, possibly they are just being considerate and giving me room with my swaying gait, certainly doesnâ€™t feel that way.

I am 25. I went in the shopping mall, nearly fell down the

escalator, I stepped forward strong foot first weak side is slower to keep up anyway I was okay. I approached the exit and saw a woman look back spot me and fully open the door and wait for me holding the door open. I was about 100 meters away! She waited for Iâ€™m guessing two minutes, again I did not think so fast and did not have the will to personally attack any with my crumbled confidence and conditioning that disabled people do not talk back so again I just said thanks. This is pathetic courtesy, sorry but how would you feel experiencing all I talk about, every day? The genes in the brain change due to environmental conditions, if you are constantly put down or degraded albeit even by well-meaning folk, your brain changes its setup, and the thoughts created by all this menial action go to your sub-conscious and effect your brain, mind and body. The sub-conscious will think I am disabled, people assume I need help with everything I better comply, the discrimination puts a stamp on your being thus a disabled persons personality with all its anxieties, behaviour is simply hardened and increased, this goes on to affect confidence and demeanour. The moral of the story: Believe me or not but I have been there and observed it in others, disability is made worse and more enduring due to ill-regard, stigma even well-wishers with petty courtesy. Pull yourself together man, it will be obvious when help is required, do not go about throwing silent insults about, you are doing more damage than you will ever realize.

The boys inner self-talk is getting more and more pessimistic, he is losing faith, self-esteem and building new beliefs about how harsh people are, the griminess of the world and his uncontrollable recluse into himself, the sad picture of his once bubbly personality, the silencing of his sense of humour, he was losing his character and this even effected his home life with family that tried to understand but reasoned his deteriorating defects with the brain-injury. He had lost all his friends, they parted in his really difficult days. He was awkward company reacting to everything unsuitably, he had nowhere to go, no-one to turn to. He suddenly fully apprehended why the anti-drink-drive message is so prevalent. He never took note or responsibility it caught him in the end, he now had to resign to feeling a fool and it being his own fault, do not complain! Look at life now, now what you going to do with it?

There is strong evidence that what a person thinks and feels has more effect on the brain than the actual environment does. What a double whammy he faces, hiding from outside influences by retreating inwards does you more harm than accepting a new dimension of reality. This will change him, the body effects the mind, so disability created new thought patterns and the mind effects the body, this is proven it is how the Placebo works, mind telling body to repair or, it can do the same for decline. Not only does he need to adjust to a new body, he has the environment to toughen up to, he too has learned new beliefs so must acquaint new inner scenarios. All this is unquestionably difficult, his mind reacts in survival mode and changes in his brain neurons, connections and cells, which in turn impose on emotions, thoughts and body to name but a few which go on to dramatically alter his person and character. The boy is me, now the man, still fighting against the mighty effects in society and in mind but I am a lucky one, I am winning. So I keep telling myself. Victory will forever remain elusive in some fields; this is why we need to start making big change happen.

What is the moral of the story? What exactly am I getting at?

How we are made and remade by forces that are largely within our control but extremely difficult for disabled people facing the great opposition of humanity. So many outer influences we tend to blame our environment. It is only how we react to that environment our inner response changes the formation of the brain which changes bodily functions. The brain doesnâ€™t distinguish between what is absolute reality and what is purely imagination. Thoughts are things, it all starts with a thought that leads to a feeling leading to action and resulting in reality shaping. Your environment will follow the feelings you have, think I am lucky, I am content, feel good and it will portray in your surroundings, with more positive encounters. Believe in a cruddy world and you will see what you believe. Hard to comprehend? I will take you on a journey, I learned to program and use my mind more efficiently, still learning but I have seen my imagination come to life, I have healed mind and body from mental-health and disability, your mind is an almighty power capable of anything. This is the story of how I learned the potency of our minds to do the miraculous and I learn the true nature of thoughts and reality. We are all connected at an energetic level.

Put simply nicer thoughts equal nicer experiences and nicer neighbours! That simple!

A disabled boy is crossing the road,

Again, he was insulted and hurt, the conditioning solidified when he told his Mother about the incidences, he faced every day, she simply assumed that, being less aware because he suffered brain-damage that he was mistaken and it could not have happened like he told. The boy kept quiet yielded and accepted yet another opposition.

I was that boy at the beginning, life seemed over I learned to forgive never gave up and after years of being close, after a mystical encounter I learned to live again, find purpose and have high hopes. I am now 40 and my own salvation has come about, how? Why? I have never felt alone on this voyage, a guiding light has directed discovery and intension, life is never ever over!

Never, ever, ever give in!

I am going to uplift you all to realize the possibilities in this Divine life of ours. Thatâ€™s right ours, there is no me or mine, simply ours or us. We are together and can unite. I will share short stories that have guided us and given hope, you remember this story it guides you to a better place of being and doing. You need not practice tempting fate like I did, only remembered the Disabled chap who spoke to us in school when I realized I had done exactly as he warned against and was now in his feelings of trying to teach his learnt lessons so they would not have to continue and claim more victims.

It has taken you long enough, you didnâ€™t want to accept the challenge, were ready to give in, but who knows when or why but you finally welcomed the light. Realizing responsibility for a life of creating you set your mind on a seemingly unsurmountable goal. To change your prescribed Destiny!

He said Iâ€™ve always seen something in you! REPETITION is an obvious synchronicity, the same comment keeps arriving in different ways, it has been long unsaid but I am feeling something at the same time. Life is taking on fresh meaning and I am accepting.

Uncovered a purpose years back, we are building up to my devastation and unveiling but it fits to tell you a little here. Had a lot of trials in life that toughened me up emotionally without me realising it until adulthood. Lost the plot fighting, drinking and drugs, became a consistent drink-driver. Had a crash. Long but remarkable recovery with lots to tell. Started volunteering speaking in schools about disability. Soon recognized I had a vital message anti-drunk-driving, expanded into colleges and other outlets, very successful should have continued but other factors reigned supreme and called a stop, I ended up in mental-health units for years, lost my purpose for years, something triggers a want to return to wellbeing with intention, do research and dig, find jewels of saviour repair myself holistically wish to share my story, a new similar bigger purpose uncovers because I can include the drink drive aspect but want to share routes to more than wellbeing, recovery, and discovery the power of mind and realities.

Will not talk much more about the distant past except when I recognize examples, living in the past is thought of the same as holding grudges, is not advisable. It makes me edgy and uncomfortable even just in writing about it because it takes my mind back there, pictures start to form and a mind cannot differentiate between an imagined scene and a real scene, this is why the placebo works, your mind effects/controls your body, your mind is suggestable, no offense it is just a fact. Tell suggestible mind something in your imagination, it cannot tell the difference of realities, the sub-conscious thinks you must want it because you are thinking about it, I am walking two paths here, mind will operate the body as if it were true and sub â€" conscious mind will create to make true, in body or the environment, minds are that potently powerful believe.

The Hills and Valleys.
ABOUT and my WORTHY GOALS
Who is involved, what is their goal.
I am middle aged, had obtrusive catastrophes that taught me a lot about life, and the recovery taught me much about our true realities.

Life lessons youâ€™ll want to teach your kids.
I record a podcast on my own, on my terms, I want and

try to make entertainment but its more educational. Will change things that cost billions in restoration.

The presenters voice and style is a message itself, youâ€™ll see why as the story envelops. Bare it out there are gems of wisdom contained.

Spiritual Freedom is my goal, the path is long and winding, multi levelled with many obstacles. Included are the lessons learnt from these obstacles, much research into gaining health but the main messages are of worldwide importance all with an essence, there are Spiritual lessons I have learnt all described. Drink-driving deterrents and disability acceptance radical reduction in the figures is as I will endeavour, a mission planted. This will make all think before they drink when they have to drive home.

I am a survivor, had a drink driving car crash. Suffered the traumas of disability and society, hospitals and rehabilitation centres, a run in with a Nuero-psychologist and my own mind.

Had a wakeup and slowly but definitely restored myself after I had my mind taken.

Spiritual freedom is my goal

Who, what, when, why, how.

A survivor of turmoil wants to teach his scholar starting now, because he does not want for others to suffer this dread so he communicates his messages speaking, podcasting, blogging and by website, determined he is to change worlds.

From a brain injured survivor who learnt to train his mind and brain, heal mental-health and dissolve disability. His message will deter drink-driving and promote anti disability prejudice/discrimination. He has a dream for the world and will ensure it happens.

Made a podcast, listen and you will never drink and drive, will grow your regard and respect and general wellbeing this needs to be in the public, I will create change.

This is highly educational and serves a great purpose, I have a dream this will be played to students, offenders and more to create dramatic changes in the world. My work is about deterring drink driving, I had a car crash under the influence. Teaching about innocent prejudices toward people with disabilities and anti-discrimination. Also mind, body and brain training, I dissolved mental health and partly a disability. Take a look, I will change societies and the world.

From driving in the wrong lane, to conquering a self he never knew.
Visual mind.
ever knew.
Childhood was a an absolute fairy tale, climbed trees and collected insects, united the whole playground to a mass game of football and won every race on sports day. Lived

with Mum and Sis, though he never realized it he missed having a Father figure to teach him vital lessons of growth. Learned all his life the hard way, it continued into adulthood but he thought these lessons were meant to get easier, instead came the hardest trial to date.

He had friends to share his time with, should regard these as life was to get lonely. He had an impeccably visual mind and an astonishing imagination, could visualize anything and he did, this made him feel with might his life was profound but he figured he was nothing special and we all could do this with our minds. Later years he would discover it was no coincidence. He was to adopt the value of visualizing for healing, it is more powerful than he inclined. Did not so much require being as suitably fitting as he was, his mind would keep him company and occupy him, from an early age he did not realise but his reality was largely in the mindâ€™s eye. He too was to unfold this truth more in decadeâ€™s time.

He has heard it best not to live in the past, does not have a wealth of memories anyway, he was so caught up in his colourful mind most of life slipped by without notice, he just remembers the poor events so its best he does not transport back. Imagination can and will take you anywhere, the mind does not distinguish between a real event and a pure imagined one.

There is little to teach about being a child, except to the elders, he wishes with his shoulders that he was encouraged more to appreciation of hidden emotive, invisible qualities, independence and other foundations of adulthood. Serious conversation was replaced with little belief and expectation, he figures he would be more today if more was expected from even the kid in him. After all what a kid learns stays with them, if they learn little that stays with them, treat a kid like a child and they will mold into your desire. He did not have social parents this effects the childâ€™s growth as well.

A want to express has always laid, as a fairly non-expressive character he has though got some knowledge to share, wisdom has grown in his years, something bound after treachery. He faced a challenge and after so promising a start in life he began by not comprehending, he was certain of his destiny, how did this appear but it was not to be the worst.

He is an adult now having badly sown seeds he reaped the harvest, but eventually he recalls the diamond seeds heâ€™d sown long ago and continues by making these prominent in thought, in mind so they will effect change.

Mind travels, Purpose uncovered.

He floated through the first part of his time oblivious to life determining dogma, he really struggled when he required wisdom but this was to grow in him.

Badly sewn seeds probably caused the reason in him to commit to searching for answers, it also led to him having to really concentrate on who he was and what he was about and this leads to purpose unveiling. He became the architect of his own identity as he was unfortunately identified by Disability after never growing up rightfully he immaturely severely injured himself.

He had a drunk-driving car crash when 21, the entry and introduction into adulthood was mangled. Because of his limited learning and other tremendously effecting, character warping incidents or baggage this was an extra test on his durability.

He met with obstacles like heâ€™d never witnessed, the crash became obsolete and not the most determining. He learned appreciation and finally regarded his mind, he did not put to use its agility until devastation infers, use it or lose it, and he lost it! This is how he learned to appreciate, he went on a self-made mission and discovered that a vibrant mind is helpful but certainly not necessary for a happy, productive and creative life.

On he goes alongside essences and advantages, solitude and stigma, he turns all his quiet time into writing and recording. His life was not worthless helping him develop into a life educator. He began talks on Disability and anti-drunk-driving, carefully using the previous as his tool to defer, this was very successful. He once proclaimed defeat, and drank lots in consolidation but he found strength and rebuilt himself entirely through self-healing. He now wants to educate the world, he so believes his work will enhance sense and wellbeing.

I always did dream of having some benefit on the world but did not know how, this was meant to be, I cannot

NOT change people in health promoting sense making life enhancing ways.

Focus and deliver

You have everything you need within your minds. Once I had everything I needed though I did not realize it when I could have made more use of these attributes, purpose uncovered after devastation enabled me to awaken to this. Found a pot of gold and continued searching. This is the partly travelled journey which has multi roads in. Thought this had near completed but an end is always a beginning. Will make you reluctant and grateful, with some envy when I was climbing to the top. You will have awakenings, remember these they will save more than just your sanity.

Have a short time to deliver several of the most important lessons a life can teach. You can take what you will gain.

Learned lots from the unrecognized aspects of gaining wisdom in my first twenty years did not comprehend the good and the bad, the heroes and the enemies had all taught me, until after conscious crushing, soul taking events and then shown the brightest beacons and near the highest heights.

The start of unconsciously preparing for catastrophe was naivetÃ©, ignorant behaviour, and unwariness though I thought I was fully competent and aware. If you are self-absorbed, you maybe will not even realize this, life passes your current bliss you miss all life has to offer, the time arrives that life and your mind will have had enough of you not listening to your instincts, emotions and intuition, let alone the signs and synchronicities of your day. A wakeup call is prescribed, will ya live will ya die, will ya pull through severely disabled and cognitively retarded, will ya acclimatize or will ya end your misery?

Yeah I was enjoying what I could, partying, socializing, and thinking of the opposite sex. Was a youth in my 21st year. Consider this I took the broad easy gate that only leads to a very winding road, I drank and I drove and I crashed very badly.

Jesus said enter by the narrow gate.
Wide and broad is the gate that leads to destruction and there are many who go in it. Because narrow is the gate and difficult is the way which leads to life, there are few who find it. Matthew
The winding road has continued, could not navigate effectively through the wide gate so will find the narrow gate very difficult. Years of disability, social distortion and unknown realities I had to learn how to live again. Coped to some extent, that was my view others said I was not coping. Love conquers all, during this monumental challenge, I found what I did not recognize until I was many a turn down the winding road, found love. Happy days in some regard. This closed and a new door opened, went away for repair, and begins the years of rehabilitation and hospitals. Mental-health of sorts tried to hinder me, many years of uncertainty. My life went from ignorant bliss to devastation. Repair to decline. In the searching for answers phase that also took years, I went through

struggles and difficulty, but once I found a small treasure I allowed discovery and enrichment.

Discovered powers that were always mine I just was not aware. This is not about what these were, that is my time what worked for me may be different for you, just am facilitating similar investigation in your own life because that is a message I want you to take. Is this, learn, grow, investigate learn grow, discover learn grow. Only did two of these that came naturally, push yourself to find more because there is a wealth of unknown skill and quantities waiting. I am not here to talk about how to walk your path, I cannot possibly, only you can do that I just am advising that it is a winding road that will have many a turn but there are sign posts of different modes to assist direction and fuelling stops of different calibres to help you grow, libraries of worldly sorts to help you learn and potential everywhere you need investigate to discover. Make this part of your life plan and the rest will fall into place. I can gently guide you onto success but only you can travel your own path and achieve, mastery is waiting many levels in attainment on route. Do you investigate and discover or do you settle and plod along. Myself I was settling the signs got bigger I continued to plod on so the sign mangled my car and nearly killed me, how much more on your lap do you want. Do you think I took notice this time?

Talk of the boy and traffic lights. The three women and road, door and bureau.

Think I am taking notice now? Our experiences change our biological makeup, it is science that environment or rather our responses and reactions to that environment alter how the brain works, the chemicals it creates and the messages it sends to the body. The party lifestyle and the alcohol started the journey that led me to this truth, not a journey anyone wants to take, you will learn and grow in your reality so you do not enter a must learn new, must grow new, must investigate and discover in a socially constricted, isolating, devastating, mind warping, stigma filled reality. Your choice, it is so easy to get to that place, it is hard lived though. Stay in your reality keep your freedom of choice, take the narrow gate and get a taxi, drink driving is a choice.

Some things are in our control, some things are not.

Fortitude requires skilled temperance to adjust. Self must love, not vane in ways because this will lead to disillusion and less awareness of reality, but love for self means a love for life can be shared. Self-love will lend a confident demeanour, confidence brings about ambition which surely motivates determination, with this comes certainty in self and onto heights of inspiration.
Love all and every living thing, we are all connected sentient beings.
Once I wrote something like sacrifice nothing, this is near impossible. For gains in any area you will have to relinquish certain traits, this is a good thing it is how change works. Make room for new gains to replace, empty

the cup before you refill.

I want so research investigated to improve, help me improve other people, lessons of my life can enhance other lives without the need to mimic trials of demoralising and destruction. I have experienced triumphs that proclaimed determination but equally witnessed triumph with lack of emotive backup. Leading to a goal only half reached. Multiple factors to consider and you must take the unknown into account. My word is taken and you will unconsciously adapt to this consideration, a single person can still gain knowledge, they are not aware of every faculty and distance a person has travelled, individuality rising, guide but never ascertain.

Anti-drunk driving is the message I found purpose in the wide easy gate, but the many directions, signs and intuitions followed or dismayed created a magnitude of wealth and discovery, but I chose a wrong path somewhere, and the dismay part took over and stamped authority. My path of gain when I was refilling the cup, changed because I had not emptied the cup of destructive beliefs, but, and this is another but, when one door closes, another opens.
This is some of how life works.

I am trying to remain more upbeat as the last piece of work I did there was a lot of moaning about injustices.

This Blog Iâ€™ll be different, that which I entertained was exactly the narrow minded albeit innocent way I used to think of disabled lives, always moaning and whinging about something. I do not want to portray that anymore. My main goal was to deter drinkers from driving, and I donâ€™t mind displaying inconsistencies as this is a deterrent itself, along with my speech and presentation. Although I learned in my writing that disability equality is an equally main goal, they both will effect masses of the world.

Heard from someone wishing to collaborate, Iâ€™m very excited, she is a creative factual writer, this fits me perfectly. Have some factual times that will come off as created but also have a story that will not seem plausible to some, I question how much of this I can release but if the essence keeps on effecting, I shall reveal all I can recall. That will make people think not only about dangerous driving but about the entirety of their lives. Think I may even want to make a film, that would be educational.

Think Iâ€™ll try my own piece of creative factual story telling:

His name is ? he always did recount the time he was told something obsolete and meaningless, they didnâ€™t stay with his conscious self for long. He never puzzled the thought that these recurring actions might mean something. Even the amazing events of his time were not considered. One day he was in the back yard on the steps listening to the birds when suddenly he had the feeling of rising up into the trees. His body hadnâ€™t moved but his line of vision was looking either into treetops or back down at himself. It was a colossal feeling that left him wonderous. They call it astral projection.

Another event years later he worked at a holiday park. He was stood on the balcony chatting with two friends, he was laughing. Actually he always did have this ability, his consciousness as he began to speak moved out to the side of him to observe himself talking, this gave him confidence he lacked because he could tell how he was presenting entirely. He thinks they call this observer consciousness.

The quality he was most happy with besides how he looked was his immense sense of humour, he thought a tough life had taught him but he did not really know where it came from.

Despite looking the part and having a top likeability and being good at creating laughter, he did not have the kind of luck he wished when it came to a lady. He did not have real self esteem just a faÃ§ade of humour and maturity, he was far from real. A true narcissist will be oblivious of himself, this makes him feel today like in his younger days he certainly had a narcissism streak, which he says under his breath somewhat embarrassed but he wants to teach others and his lifetime has many a lesson.

There was nothing creative about that, these are facts.

Have had a very Spiritual life that I never appreciated, thought I was just lucky in the Genetic lottery. I was to learn a truth that would shame and I have to live with what I was reminded and what is forever with me because other people know of this too. I once thought it would be OK if people could actually hear my thoughts because behave better, more efficiently when people, when I know people are watching me. That was the narcissist talking, I talk today from an entirely manufactured altered mind, donâ€™t imagine things you wouldnâ€™t really like. Imagination is the master key to all, if you can imagine it, you can have it. Realities in my mind came to mean more than simply imagination, I have seen wild imaginingsâ€¦ Come to life, negative ones, why I was imagining them I do not know, I was a colourful shirt! So I am thinking today, that in my vigour I had some profoundly delightful, dreamlike existential thoughts and imagination was in flow, I am just still waiting for these to materialise. Thatâ€™s what keeps me going, they are the light. All I will tell you about them is to say, God has a plan for me, I shall succeed, in some way but the Law is making it more difficult everyday. I will not go into that one.

Right thought we were being upbeat. What can you do.
Am intending a Blog, I overlap determinants that were, they are old news.
Was so creative in my younger day, if you are below 25, enjoy. When they said to me, enjoy, best years of your life just thought, sure, bet all adults say that. I say 25 because and only because, for the life I led, I never really grew up till then, also have said in previous writing, maybe because

of my own experience but I do not think we should be OK driving at 17, think more sense in an age of 25, yeah am I alone in my thinking.

Have imagined the extreme, was foretold it will come true. I however imagine differently, and still foretell my future and my destiny, anything, Anything is possible and determined thought is at the top of decision makers. Will make, am making the life I did not know until near late, but it is never to late to learn appreciation and regard.
Talk a lot about myself because I have lots to teach out of my times.

Spirituality is the biggest kept secret in the world, is that a morality issue, why does it need to be so, the enlightened few are living a very different life, of which, sure I envy, cos I was near there, but fail to see justice when I note the amount of suffering in others. I am told I am taking a purely human perspective; awakening would justify.
He began very much as a follower, though never appreciated he did not know this all he thought was that he was not leader material. Was young and silly, now he has years behind him of considerable times he has substance, some knowledge of less known things he can teach others, this gives him reason and justification to hold and lead in such a position.

Know that I have value to offer and give, will create my own employment until word gets out and parties will become interested in my service, the public is my audience I have to figure out just who will be my employer. Will serve for free to start but I want to continue in this field and refrain from relying on benefits.

Quality, quantity and spirit. Am not ready to take this out now, give me a little time, I have plans to deliver. This has become my purpose and shall derive change, wanted to proactively affect the world but will persist in delivering my lessons to the minority growing with time until hear of my work from people who do not know who I am. Spirit is the important emotive and am sure this feels right, is what I am meant to do having lost the path before. Quality is at a level I am happy with and quantity is there but have only been working with this goal for two or three days, my writing has changed and want to get a base of new material.

Personal services, appreciate the need to prepare more but want to get this public. Have enough material elsewhere but am unsure I have a solid foundation or message, though this just adds to my message without me doing any more work.

Recorded a first draft and although the perfectionist in me went back to edit to more perfection, I kind of felt good about imagining people listening, it was far from immaculate and I stubbed my toe a few times, this enhances deliverance of a vulnerable message along with what I said, have no doubt listeners will not wish to practice dangers that got me here.

Never before have I felt so much ambition certainly not with the assuredness, there is though concerns am pushing aside to continue.

Do you want a drink?

Am deciding, had clues that there is still help and that God has a plan for me. Comprehend that I will not spell out every word, I do believe have chance to make with this life something I never thought when young, did not foresee such a colloquial mission, wish I could fully get assurance of sorts.

This is phenomenal, film maker materials.

Have everything I require inside me.
Right here, right nowâ€¦
What is it I want to do?
Wish to have some beneficial effects, no matter how small scale they begin, a need to redeem my opportunity and loss. Prove myself still able to achieve great things at any level. Feel a mighty chance has flown but chances are ending, just must locate my new calling, a call of some kind is always present.
What can I do?
Can do almost anything, nothing illegal, or morally wrong, have learned the amount of aftereffect could be dealt. Can travel anywhere I wish, take any route in my reality. It is

my world, my-self and my mind make the decisions that affect myself. Intend only good to happen in me and about me, and project only intended good to others, any and all harmful, negative or otherwise bad thoughts are never an intention so they are nulled and silenced. Promote goodwill to all and negate wrongful thought, my subconscious has been through many challenges itself and activity mind did not know how to respond accurate, so was affected to follow past suggestions and conditioning and I am not denying influence from my conscious self, unskilled as it was.

What did I do and what can be done about it?
Past beliefs are in the past they no longer have mercy, beliefs are strong forces but unless I consciously agree to and fully and honestly accept a belief they have no power. They may not affect firstly me, or my surroundings. Any of civilization any territories mystical or not. Have had multiple vastly influenced thoughts and beliefs but it is only me that creates and can create anything, everything is possible so I create a repair to any and all negative in anyway bad thoughts or beliefs. Can make the future happen also can determine past influences because I believe it I am honestly and fully accepting it is possible because absolutely anything of Mystical Spiritual essence is and always will be feasible. Reoccurring thoughts are part of the challenges I faced a bigger part I put to being placed in my once very suggestible mind, any who know the slightest of mind and sub mind will be aware that a distant forgotten memory can surface given the right conditions. This is what is happening some do not choose am

remembering repressed thought/memory.

Know what me believe in, truthfully, and that suggestion can affect but will not last, not in my reality. In my reality all is perfect, a time travel back to my time of greatest wellbeing after the accident which was not all that long ago. Felt good, fabulous, walked fabulous, communicated and thought great, this time is travelling into my future to reappear alongside all added learned lessons and skills acquired thereof. Nothing absolutely not a thing is impossible in the Spiritual World we live in, and my believing Spiritual Being says I create, redeem and repair all irregularities of my true self, and take back everything that is and was rightfully mine.

What will I do now?
Thought I explained above, but justice is sometimes an awkward topic. Especially when there are rules written by many and unknown about regulations that are attached to people who cannot adhere to them or it is very difficult. Unknown laws have benefitted when was guided but where is the common ground? How do I keep these laws on my side when I am not, was not aware of the stringencies. Okay I feel I am more aware having lived through these times but there is much to remember.

A change of rule is feasible for the mighty but living on this plane with this mind it is a little incomprehensible. Fixes in my environment, the people I encounter the objects I buy and so on, were fixed to ensure my failure, yeah call me human but I find that an unfair sort of justice. Hey what is that, I am not one to talk, really, I never once asked or gave permission for my mind to be tampered with and my reality to resemble your challenges. That any person would challenge but a person recent in dramatic psychological recovery, then added to that mystical sways of identification and thinking skill, expected to complete a life altering mission with efficiency, I got close but the fixes on the path deterred direction. If this is seen through as predicted the whole scandal is immoral. I did the best I could with what I was left with. No mind, oh yeah let us challenge him now.

I will be left to discover what I can develop, I will not be harmed by any, your laws cannot oppose human rules laws and regulations. You have interfered with innocent lives unsuccessfully, I can still make success I am sorry I did not complete your hopes but obviously they did not fit my model of reality. You can you think effect so much and predict the future, why did you not ensure keys lessons were taught and life prepared me. . . oh a realization, you can do all this, you did do all this. A path allowed or catered for is exactly the one I am taking. A lesson to teach many, thanks for not respecting my life, seeing a bigger purpose and use, not asking obvious questions and assuming. I am being what we humans call sarcastic, when we pretend one thing but intend another. I am not thanking anybody for taking what is rightfully mine and doing this to me unless the predictions are incorrect. I can get used to most of this but will not settle for a certain future of prediction. I want my future my afterlife my next life, to be free to live in the grace I once had.

Will continue my work, will build an empire one day, will assist my suspicions of your goals but do not expect me to backup spiritualism, you have helped destroy me, I fight back and continue good work, helpful lessons and just watch me build an empire of kinds. I am not defeated ever.

Normality maintains even flourishes on a bright day, with features that exude quality of surreal posture. Am treading carefully, need to continue.

Medication I do not require, was other factors influencing but most of these do not affect me any longer. People cannot, should not try and determine what someone does or does not do if they have no understanding of past effectors. Judgement should not be made on what one considers best if they are far from all the actualities. Talk of different factors, if a person is away from a situation how do they possibly know what is going on. Even when in close contact people do not know all, actualities in mind, make personal decisions and should be accepted. If they are foreign to your nature learn the lingo before you make judgement. All isms are missing elements of acceptance and congruity. These lead to wrongful grasping of intention and language. We should not base anything on assumption of rightful grasping.

Write because I think will enhance others and is good for me. There are lessons to be learned but I am taken for every letter misconstrued then you project. That is not the name of why I am doing this. Thought my writing was wanted. Why are you making difficulties? You want me to be honest, tell my story? How can it be done?

I am wealthy in all categories, fitness and ability, imagination and mind agility, communicating, money wise, articulate and brilliant at writing captivating pieces of work, my skin is subtle all is perfect. I am perfect I have perfect abilities in all these.

Go on to create an empire, am very successful. No longer require benefits I support myself in the future. Am free to practice what I choose to do without it affecting anything or anyone, in my creation. I have thousands, of people involved in this empire and experts running process to serve.

Have what I need, know what I need somewhere in my mind so this emerges when ever asked

Proactive productive seamless coordinate what I write becomes apparent to myself and helpful in ways noticeable leading to good. Myself the only battle I have is with thoughts, where they originated is another story, I win thought becomes easy to decipher, follow just them that produce good. My every move does not necessarily intend other action, my every thought will become chosen if not chosen they can only be ones that are helpful to me, and enable the help intention I can offer others.

TRUTH

Iâ€™ve been saying we all are creators; people can interpret what anotherâ€™s inner world is like by looking at their outer world and experiences.

If a person is a seeker they shall find. Dreamers and creators create, believers in what they do and what they hope for make their future ambition a real possibility that is likely to occur.

Always I am seeking especially when I come against a problem area in life, and most often within days, sometime within hours, continued seeking reveals more than I am looking for. This works.

I create, I believe, that the future holds a place for me to teach the world vitally important lessons I have lived through. They do not appear to me as disasters now, refreshed outlook tells me these were a catalyst for allowing my knowledge to appear. Said somewhere that I did not learn many lessons of maturity as a child growing. Although I have a very loving Mother who supported me throughout good times and bad. Life, people and events, serendipity versus trauma were my education and I am making sense of all, just today and started flowing yesterday.

Will pass my knowledge to Billions, globally. Overall the message of hope is, we are led on certain paths to specific directions and destinations. The destination does not mean you have arrived, what will you do there, how do you think and what are your productive actions.

Take charge of your life, command what is true and what is not., you are the Master. My time has been multi levelled and tried a decline recently by my own words as what you put into the world, you shall reap. Same for your mind, sow seeds carefully. I have sown healthy ambitious seeds, there is no Law that says there is any limit of magnitude.

Old fears I had about past, strongly influenced poorly sown seeds are abolished with an inspired new mindset of turning negativity about, seeing those things as opportunity, overcoming problems to believe otherwise. Creatively visualising my desires and destiny will make for the true truth.

BELIEFS AND PURPOSE HOLISTIC FOLLOWED
Detriment began, wholistic followed, determined belief
Began life enchanted, not even middle aged and spiritually destroyed. Was this my fault. Partly but ignorance and denial allowed an added essence to influence behaviour, belief and pessimism.

Enjoyable past times were denied if to succeed. Failure was prescribed, to teach.
Was and was, I did, I sent, I proclaim. Sent a text saying some detrimental things. Behold this was to come, it

became fact. The only influence I had was the sending of this text, spiritual essences made it apparent. Not my subconscious, though this would have impacted in some way. Your subconscious hears and records all you think and speak.

Had some terrible imaginings because of this text, was in decline, they HAVE NO POWER IF I SAY THEY DO NOT. Just try and come true but I researched, prepare our young properly and learn about our minds. This can change worlds. And will.

Was told negative thoughts of mine will effect, NOT IF I DO NOT BELIEVE IN THEM AND THEY WERENâ€™T INTENTIONAL. GOD HAS A PLAN FOR ME AND IT DOES NOT INCLUDE FAILURE BEATING ME.

Raising equality has come about as an equally massive social issue. Thirdly I promote wellbeing, mind health and powers, creating and reality. These are less vital but effect the whole world. The world is my audience, need to get my voice heard. I write as well and have a vision of other companies using my work to educate and train. My reason for this is societal change globally, I started with only this goal and was intending a social business but I thought, I dream of earning my own living with my own creation of self-made endeavours.

What do I do, make, unprofessional podcast, write, used to public speak hopefully one day I will get back to this, but currently am concentrating on reaching a bigger audience via the Web, webpages and plan to individualise the categories to blogs. But need help, making more professional podcast, blogging and marketing to the globe. I have witnessed the efficiency of very successfully displaying my own disability along with telling personal stories of societies collision with me for this simple fact, disability

I continued rehabilitation by discovering and implementing self-help and healing. Improved my mind and my physical gait.

Am determined in approaching companies with large audiences, but most had the impression I was promoting business. This is a social business I am promoting so my message gets heard but have discovered I can promote to other educators that want to have a name and make good changes in the world. Will put a programme together to teach others what works and how to educate in this field. Disability equality and drink drive deterrents.

I even want to create a film or documentary, need help here. Will require funding, do not know anything about this.

This is my life purpose, help me help the world.

Hope you can help in any way.

Thanks

I am going to assist the world in people's wellbeing, train about reality creation and your mind, you are creators, you have that power. Self-help has brought me to health after a tragic near-death experience, I will put you off drink driving forever, talk about disability discrimination and society, I found this a most effective tool to drill the message home. Been am on one journey let me tell you everything I taught myself on this path back to independence including mind power and healing, the conscious and sub conscious, thinking skills and self-help, civilization and its stigmas, you will learn something.

I make posters/brochures also, am happy to help businesses, charities etcetera with design. If you can give this blog a mention, I will make this worth your while. Used to do exactly this as voluntary work, I am a natural, very artistic I really enjoy this sort of thing. I have been contemplating how I can earn a living, design and the blog/talks/cause, there is an opening there somewhere.
Get in touch no matter what you want, or with suggestions, proposals.
Keep me busy I will keep you happy.

Made a poster that I thought carried a strong message, they all do but this one was different somehow.
I had been awake the full night working on various things and for other reason so felt a bit groggy but I was so enthused I printed many copies and went to distribute, went in one pub, the perfect places to promote anti drink-driving. Spoke to the girl behind the bar just said have a look at this and decide if it is something you can put up.
She started, got half way, soon as she viewed mental health

she said oh no, no sorry youâ€™re ok thanks anyway.

I left got to another place then parked my scooter, had the thought then walked all the way back and said it is the community you should be apologising to this is a pub do you not get drunk drivers in.

She blushed and attempted to justify her response, as it happens they cannot advertise anything unless head office says so, another girl had said. Should have replied yeah so run it by head office.

I am sure they will not be so naÃ¯ve.

If we still have people of that calibre in the world, then there is certainly drunk drivers and disability prejudice, she displayed part of this.

We still have a long way to go in resolution, the more that assist me the quicker we shall get there.

Am not whinging talking so much about disability, that was back in the day, and mainly on my Podcast.

this is on many networks. This will teach a lot. Have simply found it one of the most effective tools to use to deter others from doing the same. No one wants disability, you can all comprehend where I am coming from, I know how I used to feel when looking at a person with a disability and know most of the population feel the same way.

Hold on to experiences that serve me.

Hold on to the moment, not tomorrow or later or yesterday but the moment, the now.

Go to the apparency of things, the apparent truth not the

imagined one.

The continuing trauma in the moment of now after an event has taken place is caused by stuff that I start pouring into that moment, from somewhere else not from the here and now of response. Do not start pouring yesterdayâ€™s conditioning into a reaction, make it a response and think about it and drain the moment of yesterday.

Un auto my reactive responses and just think.

What I think is happening is not always what is actually happening.

Reality is not what is happening, it is what we think is happening. We donâ€™t experience the outside we experience what is going on inside. What we perceive is going on outside.

When anything happens, anything at al, ask yourself what am I going to make of it? Your answer creates your experience of it.

All events call up past internal data.

Not only is it from my past data that my innermost truth emerges but from the choice I make of the past data I select or drape over this moment.

Mind creates my truth it does not observe. Only mind will travel back in time to retrieve every piece of data from all previous moments that resemble even slightly this moment, if it finds a match it will compare the data then add to this moment all relevant past data, thereby creating a whole new set of data and new outcome. The new outcome will not resemble the data that was originally observed. The revised additional data is hugely Influential in producing my experience of any moment in question.

STOP AND THINK TWICE.

Present surroundings are difficult for many reason. Can only centre and be present in my preparations. This is the reason I am finally doing this putting the objective and plan into writing. Unsure of the next stage in this early phase, promotion maybe or no, even better suggestion grabbing, can get professionals to ask the question to service users, this will be valuable feedback. Feedback is important, it will add to my encouragement and when I do witness audiences arriving and going away fulfilled will get plenty satisfaction, it will along with the presenting do a lot for me.

Will feel like someone in society, this is equal to motivations for starting something for others, we need to think of ourselves too. Just know what this endeavour will do for a challenged life and struggling to find any sort of purpose person. This is no small achievement and will help certainly with my feeling of worthiness. Hearing people say things like he has journeyed far. He is doing something admirable. We aspire to what he has accomplished.

It has been a few months since I realized my goal:

I am feeling very fulfilled and of use, I have witnessed people making changes using just some of methods I made use of. This was my objective and I have accomplished most if not all I set out to achieve. There has been change for the better in the community, word has spread, we made the papers and there is even talk of the news being interested on television.

I am not even thinking of losses now my goal is achieved, I had not much of a life before I set this path, so it has done multiple things- given me something to concentrate on, quite possibly led to a business so I can support myself financially, got me off benefits, and helped the community in ways I could not have imagined when things were worse, have got a social community going, we talk in the street/shops, it has been a success. Can take this to more and more people, word of mouth is good so people are interested. Not the life I envisaged but a lot better and more rewarding than the life I was leading.

 He looks at life and spies God in all.
From start to now, have travelled far.
This has been a small part of one journey but am happy with this, I tell quite a lifeline of stories thinking years back to my webpage, that got hacked and stolen but I still pay for because they have left more or less intact and it is quite a popular page. Tis my stories of the past we are at a very different today with a multitude of occurrence in between. My sole intention is to severely impact the figures of drink-drive accidents, that website is still doing a job, I am happy. I donâ€™t need credit I want truth, and know all my work when left intact will reduce fatalities and injuries.
I am truly blessed to have had such an eventful life so far, this is not the end! And I did not regard all that past me by for the first 21 years. My everything, reality/world, perception/attitude, gratitude/appreciation all were

melded by triumphant poise ignited by a secret bliss.

Feel I want and should try and recall and share a story told by a very fine man, he told of our evolution and time. We go on repeating the same story line until we get this right, with differing nuances, obviously personal choice comes into play. Unfortunately I was a little worse for ware so I struggle to recall exactly much but dribs keep popping up. . . I am sorry I donâ€™t know if I am just wishing this, hey but put into writing and is likely in my world at least. Life is a test, what your faced with how you deal with this is rewarded in some fashion when you begin again.
Oh I donâ€™t know I am honestly not spouting totally but my dream/imagination impacts the truth but exactly these directs what is truth, anything is possible!

Miracles and Divine intervention

This is miraculous nothing surprises me now, have to share an occurrence. Am a on certain enriched path that has been through trials partly my own life but influenced when my mind was acquired by others letâ€™s say.
Still believe a big influencer made some wrong moves throughout our season but nothing shall cause any unsurmountable obstacles, threw, over or past me shall complete. That me need to complete is made obvious to me and causes the production of masterful necessary work in a superior style.

Suggested track of music appeared as I was having a moment of despair, was entitled do not give up. Timing sublime as was myself just on the verge, Internet connection cut out immediately. Then my next view was do not give in. Absolutely amazing, listened and this surged me to continue, tried crying but been unable for years.

After acknowledging difficulties myself had some part in creating, forgetting my beneficial programming thoughts and nearly giving in, returned to work, there is still work to be done. Edited through the notes made and somehow my email was open, viewed something about podcast help, would you believe this was the exact editing necessary. A hacked podcast to stop advertising.

Profound.

Kept finding synchronicities that caused an emotion. My mission goes on, another placed title was changed end or something. Then inspired by thought wrote start a career, had a few topics that later emerged in email and life. Think this path has taken another twist.

Viewed the close other day, did not know near or closed, take as the latter because of resulting thought. Still plan to carry on my plight. Not giving in, had a website stolen that is still on that still advertise and pay because contains my work with vital messages carried on in a differing style today. Podcast hacked and tampered. The unfeasible has happened just to make my journey more rewarding at completion, which I add is exactly something researched and written by myself.

Something that I mention on here someplace that I was told, is revealing everyday. Would act more stunned but have written about exposure to various elements and know we all can get used to and familiar with anything.
Shall accomplish my previous desired achievement and miracle.

I am creative, am travelling a journey, have created or been offered celestial chance that continue. Though these sometimes contradict sentiment and moral inbuilt.
Moral has become, this will not end.
Trust Love this will never change, Love is the greatest protection and guide, Love to ya all.

Was made that way, but was suspicious at the events that seemed too good so denied them and was not overly suspicious at thought that I assumed were connected to memory, I should have been.
I was advised in wrongful deeds, advised of a good provider, then much later another memory, do not use this provider, please things are easier than they are being made, why do this?
Was made paranoid for needless reason, they need not have informed me of irrelevant occurrence that I would

otherwise have taken as normal
There is much in each category, including what I wrote once, which was just to teach others, not a fact I wanted to materialize. which reminds me of something else I wrote. which reminds me of something I witnessed, so this is truth, never utter a word if it is not the whole truth, negative in any way, for another purpose, not what you really want. should I continue? There is so much how the .. am i supposed to function?

Had to try a different vocabulary, altering even thought, do you know how difficult that is? What is inbred is natural, thought myself was a known self, if i am so known why did all this be allowed to continue? On the meagre hope that what you knew you knew was not truth and the opposite might materialize. so then, no one but no one ever really knows truth ay, do not deny me, I know what I know what you think you know but NO ONE and NO BODY ever knows truth, I maintain hope and faith in the one and only one.

Love.

Drunk driving facts and figures.
Some figures to put you off ever being tempted to drive after a drink.
29 people die every day in America from drink drive accidents, this amounts to one every fifty minutes. Although drunk driving has fallen by 1/3 in the last 30years still claims 10,000 lives per year, this is losses of $44billion a year due to drink-driving.

Illegal to drive with a blood alcohol content of .08, even a lesser amount can affect your ability to drive, and if you cause a crash even if you are under the limit you can still be prosecuted for driving under the influence.

Penalties are becoming tougher, tolerance is becoming less, this is really time to learn. If the dangers of injury, debilitation even death are not enough to sway you the law is going to penalize you. Jail time, fines, higher insurance, trouble finding employment, and getting college loans. If you injure or kill someone you will have a record for life that will make finding employment difficult.

Alcohol is a depressant that slows down functions of the central nervous system. Normal brain functions are slowed, you are unable to perform routine tasks critical for driving. A dramatic effect is had on information processing and cognitive skills. Psychomotor or hand eye coordination is reduced.

Judgement, coordination, concentration, comprehension, visual acuity and reaction times are all seriously compromised after drinking alcohol, does this not make sense, attempting to drive is plain idiot.

In 2016 10,497 deaths occurred in driving under the influence 290,000 were injured, someone make these figures do not let this be yourselves.

Someone is injured every two minutes in a driving under the influence incident. 25% involve an underage drinking driver.

In America the number of deaths has been cut by 50% since 1980 largely through driver education, public service announcements and tolerance levels meaning more are put off and deter others thinking of driving after drinking.

57% of deaths after crashes had alcohol or drugs in their system, 17% had both.

2in3 Americans will be involved in a drunk drive incident at some point in their lives.

In 2014 10million Americans reported driving under the influence of drugs or alcohol, just how many go unreported. This really is a worldwide epidemic, has greatly reduced in the last 30to50 years but still needs tackling.

121million times in the last year people drove after a drink this equals 300,000 incidents of driving under the influence every day.

21â€"24year olds constitute the largest percentage of drunk drivers, 30% of all accidents.

Men are more likely to be involved in accidents, 21%men are in fatal accidents 14women.

Solutions:

If you plan a drink plan to not drive, arrange to be a passenger.

If you drink any amount, do not drive, even if you are under the limit if you cause an accident you can still be charged with drunk driving.

Some states in America allow the person who provided alcohol at an event to be prosecuted if an accident is involved by one of the guests.

48states have increased the penalties for drivers with a blood alcohol content of more than .08 percent. 42 states have administrative license suspension for first time offenders.

All states have an ignition interlock system programme. Judges can require offenders to install an interlock device on their vehicle which will disable the engine if alcohol is detected on their breath. 24 states have made this mandatory for all convicted drunk drivers including first time offenders. Think this a very good route.

Here we are the second day years in but trial and error continue. This was one of my first attempts after main offer, there shall be not many more until I accomplish my true desire for the planet.

Did not write yesterday because was dark by the time was settled and did not prepare for eventualities.

Was busy afternoon, did not set out till late afternoon, could not decide if was staying or going but became apparent at the right time, my call was to go. Guess what, saw my North star again last night and the scene am sat in now is storybook sight plus how got here. This tells me made the correct decision, but did I now being sat typing history month or so.

Things were getting much back home, the insights predicted were coming to light and was not going to allow negative, harmful ones to impose.

Set out day before, made as far as bus stop, did not plan or pack good, saw sense and came home but next day after a slow start I am rushing to exit town. Was unsure but am on my adventure starting here, starting to feel did best thing, just how am going to power up, stay here until battery flat then lok for shop to locate power pack but you have to find a power source to charge them, will manage, this will all come about you watch. . did not quite happen like that.

This entry is with a different intention than my other messages, am promoting news about my work, left a file at a health centre, brought far too much heavy paperwork, so left most of this with them plus short note. My first client if you like, had many since but failed to keep diary.

Am sat against a tree looking over field, rabbits play, bird song from above, so majestic, difficult plans to make, look over check a postcard view of barn and decide thatâ€™s where to.

This is a Spiritual journey, a self-made mission in a spiritual setting, shady stats after first failure are still in my control.

Am very excited to be part of a new community and will continue with my career in life as am very passionate about society and the way you are. You have been my life since you are the one that has ever had a dream.
Will follow have edited slightly but wrote what felt at time.

New day. Tis much later still try, thought real sometime unto. Tis now unapparent, should I stay and follow, yes a new call. Had many inclination to do this, but inclined to go also. Mistakes alter ego death, think best. .already I oppose this. Stay and guide, offer strength offer Love myself to all.

Obedient moral
Beep siren replenish
Current enough even quiet
Gist win recline swill
Say winding path end shall compete
Myself written not know when
And show direct
Challenge.
Authenticity obstructed constructed
Amid issues she is at the market
Intensify expect magnificence
Brilliance redemption alliances form

Succession possession
Ahead of hour know deed
Abundances are creed
Manifest no jest
Create dreamt fate
Believe retrieve
Concentration no temptation
Supremacy fates
Are calendar dates
Connect legacy no fallacy
Wild mild cognition
Truth desire became ignition
Fallow but strength
Rise from demise
Triumph is near
Long winding path trod
Found God
Serenity in the city
Mighty mission undone
Implanted agendas
Infinity unifies
New goals accompany
Battle seems but victory beams
Rite like sleep, true to keep, own misplace, shall find grace.
Maps of meant enchant benchmark, reach and teach.
Thankya

Had a moment, thatâ€™s allowed. Nothing shall defeat am challenged repeatedly but light shines and speaks to me at the right moment inspiring me to keep going, find strength, I am strong I am love shall accomplish my desire.

Not giving in, am obliged to repair. I undo every negative thought and switch to thinking of only proactive acts of bliss and kindness, was challenged from the past but that is past that cannot affect me.

This was one path, wrong routes were trod, I now am on another path still following my ambition. Desires can be achieved so long as they remain desires.

Master the Master Plan.

Started with a plan, agenda and proactive determination. These areas supplement each other for an overall improvement in mental and physical abilities but the one main thing I want to impress, if you take nothing else from this blog, is belief is key.

Having the belief in your mind, speech and actions will enable the almost impossible, thought is equal, watch your thoughts and be conscious of what affects them.

This is where I blundered, I continued acts thatâ€™s greatly affected my thought which reciprocated onto my belief which then created.

Made a tough journey even more so, had no discipline or obedience. Heard somewhere to ignore rules if necessary if they do not fit with your model of reality, stop, is your model realistic and all encompassing, if not then this is plainly not good advice.

Believed because was from a certain place but you cannot believe and base action on what you witness no matter where is from.

Have almost failed Divinity but my mission is ongoing and Divine chance along with forgiveness and prophetic apology are allowing continuance.

Myself I improved every area of my life because I believed without question and was definite but have suffered losses as I did not continue and could not listen to my heart mind.

Have made errors in judgement that might make this sacred journey a little less rewarding, never the less I owe this work to all who witness this.

Aspects of personality
knowledge and wisdom.

Got knowledge, am wise because have knowledge, have knowledge in things that you do not want. Am wise because have done these exact things. Late maturity, drugs and alcohol, lack of regard for life, driving a vehicle under the influence.

After a drunk drive road crash, having lived with consequence, people are inviting this but trust me no one wants to learn the hard way, have strong feelings about drunk driving but I know how easily done it is. Am determined to educate have experience and knowledge of many realms of existence.

Action and power
are other aspects of personality
The action I have taken and the responses I have
witnessed make me feel good, people really
take from the lesson I am teaching so they do not make the mistakes I did, am still training others here, a bit less of

the follow though you can still learn immensely, still find power in my work not as much admittedly, looking back on past efforts brings greatness sometimes.

Miracles, miracles, this is miraculous but not much surprizes me in this Divine life of ours. Have to share what happened, am on a certain enriched path that has been difficult partly due to my own sheer mindedness but largely due to a time when my mind was acquired by another. Will not go into detail just know that this was all part of the process, that went wrong right from the outset. Still believe another big influencer made some wrong moves during our time together but nothing shall cause an unsurmountable obstacle, was expected to complete absolutely mindless so through past or over, I do the best I can with what I have, had produced some of my proudest work- without a mind.

This me to complete is made obvious to me in every possibility and produce the necessary in achievable wonderous style.

If you have doubted my lingo and punctuation at any time, am doing this on purpose, have good reason do not say some word, even myself is not fully comprehending.
Let me tell ya all, lived through loss of connection to friends and family, loss of identity, lack of emotional feeling all in the past and the test still got more challenging.

Really hope you made this far in, hope to ya all, hope myself.

challenge

Mild wild cognition

Implanted agendas

The mind emanated from the void, when the void became aware of itself.

The silent, no-mind is the void, aware of itself.

Walked through do not enter

Sometimes mystical and always life enhancing, not always apparent at the time, big lessons imparted herein started over 30 years ago.

Life is a big school, full of heroes and enemies that all will assist your growth. These lessons and the teachers are hard, but how much do you want to develop?

Have had trials and the downer years, didnâ€™t appreciate rightfully, was never ambitious, so life taught me lessons that at first destroyed me. Life also taught me that I have everything I required inside me already and to search, treasures are abounded! Learned about myself and that it is more than feasible to reach golden new heights.

Developed my mind while recovering from severe Brain-Damage, discovered truths of reality, power of mind to create and heal and the nature of society plus much on the route.

Will take you to places you have never even regarded and heights you never knew possible even in your dreams.

Learn to really look at yourself and what you do, how you

behave, how and what you think. Develop, even those who do not feel the need will be shocked at the reality bending impacts of self-discovery and improvement are.

Began with lack of direction dropping out of school then college after college, the mighty school of life little I aware, was the teacher, teaching and the education was holistic for a certain life. Relocated much in my youth, while this affected me it was not so apparent until adulthood. I learned at a young age unconsciously about facades and fronts that people including myself were putting on and how, wrongly so to oblige and fit into society. Family home life was very difficult.

We briefly talk more later. My time has been filled with lows, a prominent influencer appeared near the beginning of these and stayed, this forced adjustment inbuilt some very emotive skill.

Was low in real grounding self-esteem and never had much in the way of girl-friends but used to get on better with feminine mates. The influencer's effect on me was wariness about adult males when young, that alongside my confidence being crushed because of another reason. Health and the environment were toughening me up, but way down this path we discover that neither have to to promote the most profound distilling change, that is our minds responsibility. Mind, how or what ways we react and think has a greater impact on well-being and health than the actual environment does! There was me thinking it's a horrid society and the people are so difficult, this is not true!

Had I not seen enough troubles for a young life, obviously not because I had not seen even a blemish of the magnitude of difficulty I was to encounter. Lost the plot with health, family life, social life, forever relocating homes, unemployment, education decisions. Half-hearted attempts at suicide must have had some pronounced effect deep within my mind, would find out what it feels like to really attempt it in future years. After losing all sensibilities and becoming a drink-driver, fighting the world and its forces, which I was never going to win. Had an always on the cards car smash. Brain-Damage and Disability were my companions now, what an introduction to adulthood. Finally went for repair, this was a behind closed doors time of miracles, but another influencer influenced. Shortly after I was reborn, I lost my mind! Read on to be inspired, educated, trained and shocked. Surprised to realize life and yourselves.

This will be your beginning, a healing climb to new inner and outer scenarios.

Spiritual Lessons

This was written for my so-called amazing website; I have some of it in better form on the blog. The webpage was hacked and stolen by a mystical entity, there was loads of good stuff there, think she has just copied parts of blog and replaced.

Put this at end because am not that impressed with my thinking back then, this was a good stage, my blog is better than what she has allowed me to access.

This is a journey of rising and falling, keep becoming confident and writing I am on top when I have a setback, I am telling ya all if ya do not learn by me nothing can help ya.

Here we go then, I enjoy and find particularly useful any feedback and my biggest hope because I am limited on outlets, is to gain interest and locate establishments that would like me to present in person. It makes for a better impact, the audience seeing me hobbling back and forth in my jogging pants, the major problem is transport, am not travelling the country via public transport and taxis, my hope is to one day get this all filmed and shown on telly, can influence the whole country then. Email me anything and everything, questions, feedback, suggestions. (I havenâ€™t even begun to take this out yet, not second time about anyway. Am going to start local and see where it takes me, word of mouth will be good am sure and hopefully travel assistance or getting to a wider audience suggestion will materialize or even joining forces or hearing from someone in the know about budgeting grants/advertising/getting to a wider audience without the travel. I start with a blog.

To make clear to you that I have issues I have left this book with the abstract and errors, I mention now because there are some repeated elements to come, I think.

These are important messages so doubly mentioning is also a tool for your proper acquisition. I display inconsistencies intentionally to drive a message home without having to do anything more

A letter I wrote recently:

how do?

I observed how many visitors you got monthly a while back, but had not much content, have since had a great web page stolen, a podcast tampered with but made a blog also.

Describes an adventure, a treachery, hope, victories and denials. had a drunk drive car crash 2 decades ago, the web showed suffering society after trauma and all else entailed, the blog shows an improvement but both deliver very powerful messages.

Am confident in my work, used to talk to large groups of students and adults on drunk drive rehabilitation programmes. was in many papers on several radio stations even telly once. been through much since have written a lot, was always good with words and writing. this can change realities of drunk driver fatality and disability prejudice will lighten.

if you cannot promote my blog somehow can I at least do some guest writing on your webpage? if you do not like it or think it will not have massive effect on viewers then do not include, I include my latest snippet, a poster I made and distributed about town.

you will help save the planet from these epidemics if you embrace this proposal. I make no money from blog, there are no adverts or affiliate marketing going on, it costs me money to run, I know it can make masses of difference.

an example of a punchy direct message:

But my child is adrunk-driving easily done, hard livedbut my child is a good person.

Learn the easy way! Live and let live before it is too late. Refuse drink and drug driving.. or you can continue your learning and readjusting in a ruptured existence. Which is your favoured learning style??

Good person.

Talk of consequences, fines, bans, maybe prison, do not often include a-coma, brain-damage, hospitals for years, disability and mental-health, loss of identity, loss of friends and connections with family. Or even, maybe you would prefer death! Rebuild your persona from this!!

My life purpose, my dedication has become to promote anti-drunk driving and disability equality, get the drunk drive fatalities down from tens of millions into the hundred thousand instead. if everyone on the planet viewed all my work, we would nearly abolish this epidemic.

Your choice remember, do you not remember? You would not choose this!. . .

Want a drink? How about another?

Mind you I have learned quite a bit; do you want to enter my school? The parallel society in your new reality, some pity, some hope, a lot of patronizing and desolateness, some advantage taking, less real respect more of â€˜okay darling, nice day, do you come out often? who looks after you? who does the housework and cooks?â€™

Although there are many who fully comprehend, it is my job to make these shine as the majority even take over completely.

Want another? One more.. how about another?

sense is easy depending where you are stood, I went the

very difficult way for more satisfaction when I overcome difficultiesâ€¦ Do you want any satisfaction? I know I have the perfect answer. . . but no, actually you could end anywhere. Probably not the best suggestion but that is how simplistic all drinkers who drive when drunk is same for the drug users.

I suggest you avoid the drink and drugs and my suggestion is heard and followed.

Acceptances and denials life lessons.
Regards
please promote just this piece if not anything else, but there is a lot more where this came from.
incognito

Acceptances and Denials Life Lessons
Use this for your community group to bring a community together
Am intending to bring a community together, I had a fateful accident years back and have witnessed many greatly differing worlds since. Have been in the valley but also three quarters up the shiny light filled staircase. I accept the ups and down and appreciate I am not at my best in the recovery period. Will suggest topics of discussion having great prominence in society in attempt to improve and make these better. They are of sometimes, some of them, oblivious recognition until your denial lands you as a sufferer of them. Your real world will become

surreal, people even family will not regard what you face every day, just always remember, this is making you stronger even if you felt broken at first or still. Have faith that life is going exactly as it is meant to. Coming from witnessing the Angelic to opposing I can say I want to help, know I can but the direction is imposed.

I can and am trying, have a Blog, Podcasts, website and slideshow all describing what my denials lead to and an appreciation for obeying mighty powers and again what denial leads to. Suggested topics I am somewhat skilled in after learning the hard way: -Teach children to be grown-ups. Mature conversation is quite possible but more importantly teach morals, dignity and absolute no noâ€™s. -Do your own research on life realities, connection of all and thoughts and intention. -Drink-driving being an absolute no no, youâ€™ll regret it when you find that place in my past! -Disability equality, all of us have differing appearance and ability, in the broadest sense, it seems the wider the differing gap the more unaccepted and a forced punishment on carrying on equally in society is pushed upon. Divine experiences, the light has shined my whole life but I only noticed when this was loudest. I grow in respect and admiration. . .

Or is that jealousy? The capacity dreamt of became reality but my stubbornness spoiled one path, so I made another but because I deferred a little before I repaired the indiscernible everything was making difficulty. We are all Gods of our own reality, because I wrote I overcome any obstacle and I take the tough winding route for more satisfaction when I get to the destination it has been tough.

A quote, sorry cannot recall where from ..just because we have reached the destination does not mean we have got there and completed our journey. It goes roughly. This is an all-inclusive venture, send suggestions for topics of debate and support. Another one I have experience of is self-improvement and self-healing, mentally, emotionally and physically. Belief and faith played a big role here, these are two most powerful words. Drink driving is the preferred UK term for driving under the influence of alcohol.

The US equivalent is drunk driving, driving under the influence (DUI) and driving while intoxicated (DWI). Statistics (UK) 10% of all accidents with injury are caused by excess alcohol; 33% (66% if between 10 pm and 4 am on Friday and Saturday nights) of all drivers and motorcyclists killed have blood alcohol levels over the legal limit. At double the legal limit, the risk of crashing is 20 times greater than that of a sober driver. What do we think of drivers who are drunk? There is growing disregard is there not? Find yourself in situations I have been in and you cannot refuse it was your own doing. Lost friendships because of lost identity, awkwardness, inappropriate reactions, disability, mental health. Court, fines, bans, prison even death is not enough of a deterrent, we have to teach with upfront honest words.

Used to educate talking in schools and colleges about the drink and driving and one lucky survivor consequence called disability. I hope to get back to the public talking, this is my continued venture to educate the world.

Disability there is no amenable word is there? Infirmity, disablement, impairment, defect, disorder, affliction, handicap, disability. I strongly disagree with the current word, you do not dis-the-able and you certainly do not dis the afflicted.

I invented a phrase years ago.. Missability, because of how most of society think it politically correct not to even make eye contact. Do not stare.. They cannot help a glimpse at your feet though as you stagger or a quick shifty up and down glance. Or they jump back ten feet a flap their arms in giving you right of way, drawing attention is most unwanted.

Drink and drugs, like I said I wish this to be an inclusive sect, we will draw worthy sentiment from the drug user as well as the parent to the poorly child and the Divinely inspired, all are welcome, do not judge me even if you have foresight and I will not judge you.

This day
You can judge from the pitch of my tone throughout that I have had highs and lows and maybe relapsed a little as we have gotten here. I started another webpage which I was very happy with but I had some minor difficulty, went back to my other one and the whole index of pages had been deleted!

I face turmoil but do not let them win, the pages were still intact online so I made a little rescue, as it happens this all worked out because I scraped together the five pages of my new page and placed them as a good start point gathered the other, which was getting lengthy put them all together. Now I think I have something of real value to you.

A lesson for you all, I stopped exercising so much, started drinking no drugs but I am back on meds. Had an episode, I am not proud of at all. Synchronicities tell me it did not go unnoticed.

Am forgetting stuff, not as focused on my writing, get lots of blocks to my work but think you will like this latest, all made sense to me.

But it is not me I have to get through to. There is about four or five hours of material from three webpages together, some is repeated I think but they are important messages. I listened on a text to speech engine at quite a fast pace as well. Am going to do something with this for sure.

Am not feeling great was up all night again traversing one block after another obstacle, I know what you're thinking and its true SO take heed, I have done this to myself with the added outer influence that would have backed me if I did not go off the track from day one. Am not taking full responsibility for that, some may think I should but put the shoe on the other foot and check my skirmishes that's if you even know the whole story as it happened. Surely, I am wrong, the Divine does not make mistakes but I always knew something major was going to go off in my life.

You will not find a more friendly enemy. The comprehending of my metaphoric speech. Yeah, that is another thing that I did not do, elocution lessons, my accent, my slang, my lingo half of this need not have been. I am not totally denying responsibility just there is no way I own it all.

Am putting my efforts into starting to earn myself money now, but am late on the uptake, surprise.

Will battle on oh I could have had it so good.

Satisfactory, productive and benevolent life.

Everyone deserves rehabilitation trauma or not

Remember in rehab the psychologist telling me how even the healthiest person can benefit from rehabilitation. It is all about teaching you to live to your best, even without trauma we can all do this.

Make small changes, witness big difference. A farmer drives his tractor to the cow field every day to feed them. He does this for twenty years, eventually the path to the field is grooved with ruts from the tyres so he does not even need steer. But say he makes just a quarter inch turn on the steering wheel then the tractor ends miles away from the centre of the field where the ruts lead to.

As when I was in rehab, early days I did not comprehend how just simple talking with this, later realised very smart bloke was going to help me recover. The thing he was interested in and the questions he asked seemed insignificant to me back then. Was all due diligence and it helped him understand how I worked mentally.

I was in a very vulnerable, malleable state and he got to know me, which is when I thought it all a waste of time then he utterly crafted me back to better than I have ever felt. It may be mentioned later, just wait there is more to come. You will get a sense of something more than sentimental throughout.

All facets should be considered

Just want to emphasize the scale of work and determination, all be it unskilled that has gone into a calling. This is a demonstration of will and great obstacle climbing, internal and external, recovery and realized life, mystical and evolutional.

While this writing goes on and while at times I peak and visualize my future as a success, I am not totally content. I feel I am making errors mystical in nature I will not go into detail but just know I am going through trials at the present time, no matter how I sound. The mammoth failing that so hindered me affected everything, so still I question what I do, how I do it, when I do. I was foretold a future that burdens every move, every thought. So do not think I am on an ego trip and living in cuckoo land, I am demonstrating willpower of kinds, to not be defeated, to ignore if necessary if deterrents do not allow my plan to emerge, and still aim for my goals.

My metaphorical speak of hero and enemy. My own or my own influenced thoughts are just some. You see I am in a battle to conceive a destination. I have, no they are not always an enemy but since the turning point, they have certainly made me aware of presence. Now I do not know whether these are human malfunctions or mystical, I suspect the most, they are humans with mystical qualities. Whatever but I am still not convinced if they are trying to make difficulty or guide me to backtrack.

Occurrence has taken place that I expected, are these mistaken imagined memories? The main difficulty I face is in me, my thoughts, nothing solid. So, I am of hopes that I have just been programmed to think a certain way and none of it is truth.

Respect

Do you #consider all things? Do you #respect all people, all things, all of life? How about yourself? I must reiterate, I am not preaching, these are the potent #lessons of my life and what knowledge I have gained during my short research years. I am in no place, I am not one who can dictate to others because I live with regrets and failures, these have taught me. I learn the hard way, share my trials so you may learn by me. By your research you come across these words and they will forever stay with you and alter bad habits making for productive change to your persona.

I had great respect for some of the wrong things, minimal respect for a few of the right things but thought I was doing fine. Thought I was an individual with emotive talent that made me correct in most situations. I did not succumb to an opposition in opinion, whether this was advice or suggestion from friend or foe, I was right. It took rehab to identify and help me recognize the narcissist streak in me.

Do not get me wrong I was mostly content with my character but a narcissist will not even spot fatal inconsistences, even be skilled at hiding them. Upbringing is the foundation for developing attitudes. For family and health reasons and lacks in certain areas I grew with few character building rules, and made my own to fit comfortably with my developing ego.

Talk to children about their feelings, thoughts and fears, you will get more sense and effecting dogma than you may realize. A considerate deep conversation is quite possible kept to a juvenile lingo and will have profound effects on the growing childâ€™s ability to communicate and operate, it would too bring you into a real closer relationship. I have trepidations, I am talking like I know when really I do not, I am no psychologist or expert I have not even got my own kids and I am lecturing about child rearing. How can I possibly know what is best for different families? I do not, I base all I say on my experience and what I now know lacked. Which I know partly taught me the nucleus of wide uncommon knowledge or maybe I am thinking too much so, that my experience was like no other, there will be similarities that imitate to degrees and there will be those who can grasp what I say and those that say you did not see nothing you want my life!

Lives are different with included same nuances this is why I can put ideas out there. All the relationships I had lacked substance and were often fronted with facades of all kinds. You will be overwhelmed at accepting a child can often sense these and it effects their behaviour even when they do not know what the quality is or what it means, they will be determined by those invisible forces I mentioned earlier. As I said, now I have demonstrated my reasoning, all forces invisible and the like should be taken into consideration.

Prevention and cure

A colleague did some web searches on one of my topics, drink driving. She pointed out that there are very few approaching the subject from a prevention angle. What do they say? Prevention is better than cure.
She said there was a lot of what happens after you are caught or caught out, solicitors, rehabilitation.
This is a course of rehab before the event takes place, this

will determine your sense and where we are all so sure we will take it careful and be ok all it takes is something in the road.

I am in no doubt because I have worked with both and witnessed recovery on day one from my work, that this blog worked through will sway you more than rehabilitation. I find that description a contradiction I have been to rehabilitation, Neuro rehab, these so-called rehab courses are not making people better, they are only there to reduce their conviction.

One woman on a rehabilitation course I was introduced to and told I would never make her better, she is always here. I saw her in town I was with my Mum, she sincerely said thanks so much you made me appreciate, I am never drink driving again! Prevention and cure! From the first hour of an expensive week-long course!

Today I had an important meeting about my work, I travelled about two miles on my mobility scooter, it was snowing, a few inches settled during our meeting so I left early and went slower on my way home. Still, I skidded going at snail pace, well it was more like a slide, I kept turning and sliding the opposite direction and near went down a curb into the road.

This was dangerous, and I was sober!

People I find that are in extreme positions tend to appreciate hidden qualities or maybe just the small things and seem to connect. There is an unspoken of comprehending from both sides.

The homeless have been a constant in life since my accident, at first when I was really unwell, they were amongst the few that would always talk to me in a non-derogatory way. Then I found it easier to talk to isolated people with less social acceptance.

Next town I approached someone at a social gathering who was sat excluded from all by himself, he became my best friend, he was homeless at the time, he has got a place now, I wish him all good.

Next town, I let this approaching strangers take lead, I had had a relapse mentally and was keeping all sorts under my roof, anyway I learned the hard way and went back to my old non trusting manner and stopped this. A while later I became friends with someone who became homeless, I will not even trust him enough to offer him a bed but it is not practical anyway, we get along fine as thing are. He needs to warm up, I need the companionship so we all gain. I still feel trodden on though by some of my so-called mates, nothing will ever change for some people, I am just waiting for this superior life that I definitely programmed.

I will change worlds, need assistance because I am getting nowhere on my own.

I am able, more than able to change statistics for the best, this has become my life, I am not earning from this and relying on benefits, it needn't be this way

The Placebo is real

Drinking.

People are shocked, how can I still drink when this was

responsible for my near death. Even I am not sure, replace with something else, I have accompanied this but feel the time has arrived to stop.

Spurred on by a mate who has drank for years, he wants to drive again, did not trust himself while drinking so definitely decided to stop. I said after a few minutes, we'll do this together.

I was in a much better place the last time I quit drinking, I am in that good place, doing some good work that will only get better without the alcohol.

He said alcohol is killing him, he wants to visit his Grandchildren. I am eager to find that self again that feels and thinks better, here I am lecturing about how drink changed my life and get told by someone that drink is ending him, so I have been told as well to practice what I preach.

I believe in my work so much to have stamina to effect for the good, I know I have witnessed this so I am going to enhance my messages and stop drinking again, if I can you all can.

Drink has been agility burden all my life, got in fights because of drink, crashed my car because of drink, failed at various things, lost relationships and effected health because of drink. This is about time to learn do you not think?

I will keep you updated. . .

First night: I am not going to lie, I have a few beers in the fridge, I will have some tonight but intend not to buy anymore, he said he has a bottle at home and is isolating himself for a bit this will help him.

Language of your mind

What you think may be just as harmful as that you do physically, so repair all them bad thought you had, now. All you need do is readjust them in your thinking repeatedly and soon enough you will acknowledge structures, whatever they were, redeeming in your surrounding or maybe they are in your mind. All I talk of has been tried and tested by myself and believe I did not enter voluntarily, I found myself in a destitute place so I researched my pants off and dug myself out of that hole, still climbing but I am a climber.

Have no bad thought about another or an argument or situation of conflict, this can only add to the bad feeling, you will think good of the worst situation, you think good of your enemies and before you know it, they are your friends.

Only think about truth, it is true that you can accomplish absolutely anything with your mind. Only good thought shall enter and remain, negative thought is replaced instantly with pro-active good feeling thought. Go on, test my hypothesis, do this repeatedly enough and you reap the benefit even if they seem different to the original thought, thou must learn the language of the mind which is different to the language of the sub-conscious mind, which you must also learn.

The most successful, richest, prudent people know all this, why do you think they got to where they get?

Hope you are driving your life, how do do go on the road? Do you ever tempt fate? That one time could be enough. Speeding, drinking/drug driving or are you just plain reckless? You can be as careful as you assume, no-one can stop what is going to happen if you keep this going. Drink/drug driving, speeding will catch you out in the end. Hope no-one is, well if anyone is hurt is only fair this will be the irresponsible driver.

Someone just told me about her sons, a story which I connected to dangerous drivers. some like one of her boys thinks only a minimum into the future, doesn't really contemplate all. This I relate to those drivers who are not even contemplating the worst consequence. The other debates ten years into the distance, this makes for careful, I bet he is a careful driver. Consider, do this now, consider what your life would look like in ten years if the bad did happen? Accident & Emergency and early rehab for five months, loss of identity, friends, connections in your cognitive malfunction for one year before you go to rehabilitation for another year, then you end in psychiatric unit for six months, move town, isolated, brain damaged, now with mental-health on top. Another year goes by, you cannot handle things, they put you on stronger medication, this works, gets you on an even keel so you think I do not need meds so you stop, relapse, back in hospital for another six months, you come out only to be used by all the scrounging you attract, you start drugs and booze again. Hospital for a year, move out into yet a new home because you lost the other, do not like things where you are so move street, then get evicted, third house in two years. Used, taken advantage of used some more. Ditch the users, isolation is your friend now, five years of few visitors and desperately trying to get your story heard, you can save others, they saved your life now what you going to do with yourself?

She also said she does not allow herself a drink if she has to drive the next day. Now that is sense. Responsible I said. Take her lead you may just thank her story one day. She does this because she lives out of town in a village so needs her car to get to and for work, no car, no work, no wages, no bills paid. Her life would totally tip if she lost her license, do drink drivers contemplate all this? No, it is all about what punishment could I get? Oh, I will be fine, you want punishment? Live this- A-coma, loss of consciousness, wake to not know who you are or who your Mum is, fit into society with a muddle of a mind like that.

Why do people drink and drive?

The placebo is real

We can all improve our health, illness, disease, mental equity, physical prowess with just our thought. Top actors, sports men and women, business people all know this. It is in their daily routine, for some this is part of their training.

Heal the mind, heal the body. Train the mind, train the body.

Athletes get faster, golfers and other sports players get better scores just by using the power of thought, no practice just thinking and visualising. I improved a physical disability; my gait was so much smoother and mentally I improved just by visualisation and imagination of my imagined ideal truth.

Film stars use the power of mind to remember more lines, some have successfully used this for gaining more wealth. They write themselves a check, look at this everyday and imagine it has happened, they visualise how they have spent the money, new car new house, imagine yourself behind the wheel, sense its colour, sound of the engine and exhaust, smell of leather upholstery.

Here it is important to be grateful, this is a most vital sentiment almost in line with faith and belief, thank your coach or tutor, be grateful for family, health, shoes on your feet, air you breathe, there is always, always someone worse off than you are. Gratitude will come back to you tenfold in various disguises.

Friendships.

Love your friends, they are precious. I had plenty when I was at school or college but I did not fully regard them until I moved house to a far-off town, then the accident and isolation encapsulated me. Things, your life, your mistakes, your hopes are all assessed like you have never thought about them before, your dreams are shattered while every negativity looms. Bad memories are easier recalled than pleasant ones. Every time you catch yourself have a bad thought or negative memory catch yourself and replace it with the opposite kind, every time. your subconscious think you must want what you think about most often so takes action, this is cancelled out by a pleasant one, you will never get depressed.

Upbringing.

Did you know that if you have got not very social parents that can affect you? You are going to have to push yourself to be different from them, chase relationships of all kinds, get outside of your comfort zone, life begins at the edge of your comfort zone.

Drink driving has risen in 2015 to highest levels since 2009, there has been sharp decreases but during this epidemic this has struggled. What I have said that some will not learn through fines or prosecution- more than 5,000 drivers were caught drinking twice in five years. 450 were prosecuted twice, 2 were caught six times. 219 received endorsements once, 8,068 were caught twice, 449 were caught 3 times, 46 were 4 times, 5 five times and 2 six times! This is why I know my work works, hardened hardcore offenders admitted after event to learning and assuring they would never drink drive again after my first hour of their week-long drunk driving rehabilitation course.

The Guardian said perhaps it is time to review some of the medical checks and rehabilitation courses before allowing these drivers back on the road. This I agree with, one lady I met on a rehab course was a regular, she was not there to learn, she was there for a reduction in fines and ban. It took me 1 hour speaking to make her realize how lucky she is and not to drink drive, another had tears in her eyes thinking again how lucky she'd been to not end in my situation.

I am out of practice but intend to get back to the talks, I have some especially influencing personal stories of society interacting with me and my disability.

I am trying my best to promote via web, public advertising making posters and everything, I have even emailed local Member of Parliament. I cannot understand why more are not jumping on board in support. I am going to two police stations, multiple colleges and sixth forms to promote. Determination is key!

Does the advent of self-driving cars allow for drinkers to drive?

Short answer no but there is controversy.

Can the growing times be responsible for eradicating drunk driving? With the invention of self-driving cars could liveâ€™s be saved every day? Because in theory the introducing of driverless cars would banish the great risk of drunk driving, right?

Can a person ride intoxicated in a self-driving car is a topic of debate, exemption is clear cut for fully automated vehicles, not all of them are fully automated, there are six categories which are:

Level 0. No Automation: The human driver does all the driving.

Level 1. Driver Assistance: An advanced driver assistance system (ADAS) on the vehicle can sometimes assist the human driver with either steering or braking/accelerating, but not both simultaneously.

Level 2. Partial Automation: An ADAS can control both steering and braking/accelerating simultaneously under some circumstances. The human driver must continue to pay full attention ("monitor the driving environment") at all times and perform the rest of the driving task.

Level 3. Conditional Automation: An ADAS can perform all aspects of the driving task under some circumstances. But in these circumstances, the human driver must be ready to take back control at any time when the ADAS requests them to do so. In all other circumstances, the human driver performs the driving task.

Level 4. High Automation: An ADAS can perform all driving tasks and monitor the driving environment essentially, doing all the driving certain circumstances. The human need not pay attention in those circumstances.

Level 5. Full Automation: An ADAS can do all the driving in all circumstances. The human occupants are just passengers and need never be involved in driving.

If your hands are not detected on the steering wheel the

car will sound the horn, if continued it will put hazard lights on and slowly come to a halt.

Level 5 vehicles (Full Automation) likely will not be available for the public for some time is probably being optimistic.
Many websites and articles have even claimed that in the future, driverless cars will allow drivers to drink well past the legal limit and just have their cars drive them around! Though the name â€œdriverless carâ€ would give you the impression that this would be possible, we doubt this will happen anytime soon.

Self Help Alliance

Unrealistically and not given a look-in I used to think, in my naive younger years, that self-help was a market for the needy looking for some manufactured kind of so-called assistance, now after years of becoming that desperate person and giving self-help a chance, I have come across many successful anecdotes and like so many others have true belief in this, one of the biggest niche markets.

Will just mention the few more productive ones as also memory does not always allow me to recapture.

Visualization, I had immense success with visualization. You mind can and does instruct your body on biological operation and purely physical performance. So loosening up a previously hitched up locked in hip was easily done.

Believe me when I say I made my walking the best it has ever been and without much exercise! I remembered the exercises in rehab and what they intended and just by visualization was in fact carrying out these exercises. I recalled instruction telling me to extravagantly swing my hips while walking, the exaggeration imposes a return to natural movement, this worked just by imagining throughout the day.

I imagined walking with a swagger and flowing onto the next step. This works, it is one of the most fascinating treatments, athletes use for training to optimal levels. Golfers improve their par; sprinters improve times just with visualization. There are fascinating stories across genres revealing the simplest way to achieve optimum performance

Ask the universe

Was mostly content most of my life, well far from really for multiple reason but was a camouflaged happy. Something was still missing but this remained elusive, until middle aged this was hidden partially revealing in increments.
Core beliefs, my true nature and self have fronted unrealized goliath powers which were redirected, I am still learning and slightly opposing but the opening of a new phase is mine and I am becoming complete, am creating supreme concepts.

This is my attempted resolution to figuring out my reality.

Learned to keep exempt anything less than a good intended word, my reality is shaped by this, we all have this ability I am just working out magnitude.

Social integration is main, for various lessons I have travelled through spheres of acceptance and seclusion. Sustaining inclusion has become less easy through my own creation, so I can make that ease reappear. I am opening to and expanding my consciousness I am cultivating no less than my best brilliance.

Choose to regain full control over my thoughts, actions and speech in a truly acceptable way. I am so articulate and always have ample to say.

The way I work best is to have conversation that gives me opinions. I have vast opinion about some serious topics so try me and speak, ask questions, tell stories, give me your worries and I will resolve them but you must listen and take action.

Face this or not but the younger you are the less experience you have of cause and effect, the effects can be massively affecting.

I yearn for this state of pure clarity
What is true I wish revealed, I know my truth
Love is forever
I love knowledge
I believe
Am pro-creative
Illusion will ultimately be unveiled
love perfect thoughts and intension in perfect harmony

Compensate chemicals
Survival exhibits

Drive, thrive and stay alive, derive to arrive and drive sensibly.

Twenty years ago, my life was altered, cannot believe this much time has passed. When people say to the younger generation enjoy your years because before you know ages will have gone and the hours pass by quicker, this is really the truth that I admit to not appreciating until too late but I would never want to rewind, maybe to change my ways during these life alternations but I would like always to return to wiser days.
Having had what I then considered uneventful later I appreciate with hindsight very differently, I have had a fair few life changing episodes that when added together make for or seem to make a very filled eventful life that I learned greatly from, this I hope is evident that the reason why I talk about my past is not to grandeur any of this or gain such things as sympathy or admiration if you will but to train others, we can all learn from anothers experience, this is partly why the autobiography industry is so popular, call this biography if you want I am not approaching with that intention. I am confident when I say even adults can learn from what I say because I have witnessed this and had many an aspiring word said to me.
I am focusing.
Getting back to drinkers, and relinquishing from my goals. You are not interested in me probably less interested in my aims and story so I feel with lost mind, the right thing to do I just hope you are still with me. I am getting there, just

hope you are all still with me.

Saying if you live, if you do not end in jail, if you do not kill anyone, you will be so cognitively retarded at least at first, your friends will lose interest in the person they got to know.

You will appear pathetic to them. Drinking and driving is a pathetic action that is only asking for any one of a number of things, all detrimental.

Drive, thrive and stay alive, derive to arrive and drive sensibly.

Get in contact

Ask me questions, post your feedback and comments or stories, I will include the best on my blog. I love to hear from people and what they think.

Have a think

This has been a real preventor, I truly believe that law does not affect, that's proof that people still drink drive. Personal stories of what drink driving can so easily bring or worse tend to have better affect.

Remember drink driving is so easy for a reason, that its catastrophe can be immense. Easy things bring the most adverse effects, the moral amongst us would not ever

drink drive. Are you a moral, upstanding citizen?
Think of other road users, think of what you could put your family through. My mother had to give up work to look after me. Just think, have a thought.

This is real prevention and cure for drink driving

Want a cure to drink driving? This will work. My history involves drink driving and my ongoing future is deterring drink driving.

Personal stories of disability and society and realities will affect you more than laws, guaranteed.

Try this

Every trip out was filled with horrors that society found acceptable. I hobbled to the traffic lights two girls started laughing loudly at how I seemed, oh well they were young. Then a teenager passed me but came rushing back, brushed passed me just to press the button on the crossing for me.I carried on,

then a woman coming toward me looked up saw me shook her head and crossed a busy road instead of pass me on the pavement. I carried on.

I was in town with mum, went to the voluntary bureau, the woman looked at me daft, I hobbled over after nearly falling over, ask her a question and unbelievably she swung her chair round and shouted the answer to my question at mum who was stood near the entrance. I carried on.

Nearly fell down the escalator in the foyer, five minutes later I was exiting, I was two hundred meters away from the doors, a woman looked back saw me coming and fully opened the door and held it open for me. Insulting, I got in I can get out. I carried on.

Just outside the very same door I tripped and stumbled a little, a man saw this and came over with a glutton look on his face, he asks me for a cigarette, I said no, he then gave me a sob story why he urgently needed money for the train, I said no, he asks for something else, I carried on.

Can you not imagine every trip out including all this and other detrimental behaviour? Your subconscious will listen as you say thanks to the boy for helping with the button or the woman helping with the door and think you must want this treatment so it changes you internally and externally, fact, it is science.

Well-meaning well-wishers unknowingly harm you as much as scroungers or ignorance, I really hope I am educating, you will know if your being wrong or if help is really needed.

Can you not put yourself in such a situation? Disability discrimination has many faces but a lot think that they are being nice.

accepting and acknowledging your perfection

The truth will set me and yourselves free, you'll experience the frustration of the same circumstances until the desire for answers and change outweigh this.
By understanding, accepting and acknowledging your perfection you offer yourself this experience.
You cannot know what you truly need to learn until you go through the necessary, often uncomfortable experiences.
There is power in faith, true wisdom comes not just by getting older but by experiencing truth.

Why Do People Drink and Drive?

The answers will stun.

-More than 1 in 10 millennials believe they could drink more than the legal limit and still drive.   This may be true for half a mile but how much lowered efficiency do you want to tempt?

-40% let friends drive drunk because theyâ€™ve done it before.

I have heard people say things like, I always do this and I am fine. There comes a time, this is called regret, live with disabilities have you? Want to try it?

-20% of men and 7% of women would let a friend drive drunk to avoid an argument.

And I thought men were more assertive! Your not much a mate to not consider the potential catastrophe.

-Booty calls: 1 in 4 drunk drivers are headed to a â€œhook-upâ€ location.

Sex on your mind. Yeh I remember my youth, check how many dates you will not arrange because your mental-health and/or disability scares neighbours, people in the street let alone one to flirt with!

And hereâ€™s how the age groups of survey participants broke down:

31% were 18 -19 years old. Young at heart, young in mind, its each generations job to educate and teach the coming generation.

15% were 20 â€" 36 years old. 21 - 24 year olds are the majority.

62% were 37 â€" 52 years old. Wheres the wisdom of your years?

Adopted an invisibility cloak

Potentially I will save lives and prevent lunacy and dismay.

This is going to be eventful, have many ideas worth sharing. Am pleased I found such a role as to teach in four main areas, the first two, you may consider yourself exempt from but listen in. They are -drink driving, why have we not learnt? 27.8 million Globally admitted to driving under the influence. Does this shock you? Does to me and I was one in this statistic in my immaturity, was 1point from brain-death in a-coma due to a drunk-driving crash, becomes a passion to deter this disgrace. Used to talk in many venues, -Disability education in schools was how I started, moved through the colleges and onto a road safety offenders rehabilitation program. Disability prejudice is what I am targeting today. -General life appreciation, the life of discrimination and disfigurement lead to me searching for answers and appreciating the small qualities of display in people, life gems, family and friends, health and healing. This opened many doors and -powers of mind or -reality creation became prominent in my life. This is self-help like youâ€™ve never witnessed. Equality and sense have more meaning to me now and it is something I can effect. I want to make my work into a career, nothing will make me happier.

It is my liberty and in my power to inform and cultivate, prime, nourish and nurture, and enlighten the people. You are feeling as excited to be here as I am. Interest and will, I can influence, we start with the tyrannies of society, social reason and control and constraints, we will echo freedom for us all.

Deductions.

Adopted an invisibility cloak to some, the community felt they were being correct by not drawing attention or even looking at me or they were intimidated, why education is needed. Or an abusive sticker on my forehead, so many passers would grimace at my uncomfortable gait, actually they would not look at my face but often glanced a stare at my legs/feet. Or money symbols floating over me, the scroungers come out to play, they have no self-restraint or regard and find vulnerability an easy target.

Minorities and majorities controverted. What do you care about? My cares have shifted: The unobserved is destroying millions of lives, crushing the wellbeingâ€™s of people with Disabilities, all the above is demolishing neighbourhood spirit and deeply affecting others.

Drunk driving facts and figures.

Some figures to put you off ever being tempted to drive after a drink.

29 people die every day in America from drink drive accidents, this amounts to one every fifty minutes. Although drunk driving has fallen by 1/3 in the last 30years still claims 10,000 lives per year, this is losses of $44billion a year due to drink-driving.

Illegal to drive with a blood alcohol content of .08, even a lesser amount can affect your ability to drive, and if you cause a crash even if you are under the limit you can still be prosecuted for driving under the influence.

Penalties are becoming tougher, tolerance is becoming less, this is really time to learn. If the dangers of injury, debilitation even death are not enough to sway you the law is going to penalize you. Jail time, fines, higher insurance, trouble finding employment, and getting college loans. If you injure or kill someone you will have a record for life that will make finding employment difficult.

Alcohol is a depressant that slows down functions of the central nervous system. Normal brain functions are slowed, you are unable to perform routine tasks critical for driving. A dramatic effect is had on information processing and cognitive skills. Psychomotor or hand eye coordination is reduced.

Judgement, coordination, concentration, comprehension,

visual acuity and reaction times are all seriously compromised after drinking alcohol, does this not make sense, attempting to drive is plain idiot.

In 2016 10.497 deaths occurred in driving under the influence 290,000 were injured, someone make these figures do not let this be yourselves.

Someone is injured every two minutes in a driving under the influence incident. 25% involve an underage drinking driver.

In America the number of deaths has been cut by 50% since 1980 largely through driver education, public service announcements and tolerance levels meaning more are put off and deter others thinking of driving after drinking.

57% of deaths after crashes had alcohol or drugs in their system, 17% had both.

2in3 Americans will be involved in a drunk drive incident at some point in their lives.

In 2014 10million Americans reported driving under the influence of drugs or alcohol, just how many go unreported. This really is a worldwide epidemic, has greatly reduced in the last 30to50 years but still needs tackling.

121million times in the last year people drove after a drink this equals 300,000 incidents of driving under the influence every day.

21-24year olds constitute the largest percentage of drunk drivers, 30% of all accidents.

Men are more likely to be involved in accidents, whether this means they are more likely to drive after drinking, I think this is the case. 21%men are in fatal accidents 14women.

Solutions:

If you plan a drink plan to not drive, arrange to be a passenger.

If you drink any amount, do not drive, even if you are under the limit if you cause an accident you can still be charged with drunk driving.

Some states in America allow the person who provided alcohol at an event to be prosecuted if an accident is involved by one of the guests.

48states have increased the penalties for drivers with a blood alcohol content of more than .08 percent. 42 states have administrative license suspension for first time offenders.

All states have an ignition interlock system programme. Judges can require offenders to install an interlock device on their vehicle which will disable the engine if alcohol is detected on their breath. 24 states have made this mandatory for all convicted drunk drivers including first time offenders. Think this a very good route.

Some on a night at the weekend will have more than five drinks, two drinks double your chances so four drinks quadruple them so five or more and you are asking for trouble.

Would rather have paid ten times a cab ride home than the resulting 20 years. Need to use cabs a lot these days, cannot drive anymore, the left vehicle is your choice, the other three are no choice.

Good night out? You will have more than a head ache if you wake up in the morning.

Never drink and drive.

You do not need to be drunk to be at risk, just one drink increases your chance of collision. You had so much going for you.

Repeat after me; I recall all these messages, forever.

Drinkdriving@preventioncure.uk

Update; I have been through much, even lately, have not started the things I was aiming at. The hovering presence above all this writing being the reason.

Have said much I truly felt at time but thought changes, attitudes shift.

My half mate tells me he has not seen me smile for the past3 and ½ years, if I am honest, I do feel like crying. Iâ€™m not out to mislead any, if you want to try this rollercoaster, keep drinking or the drugs will do.

My failures demonstrate just a single life of head-injury, and I am a lucky one! Brain-damage can and does affect different people in a million differing ways, in fact just a million hasnâ€™t enough digits to categorize!

I hope I portray my scattered self, this book is a deterrent, my style and actions or lack of and dreams that came to nil have demonstrated, you will not enter this place, you have sense, you live a long healthy life.

Please email me comments, if Iâ€™m not writing I will be answering emails. You need any more convincing not to try this? My lifestyle full of sorrow and shame is so easy accidentally apprehended.

email; drivealife@protonmail.com

We have an abrupt end, do you want finishing?

Drink/drug driving or speeding is an abrupt end indeed!

I have intentionally left, what I call my abstract impression to help deliver a message. None of this book is abstract! Is all fact, let this be an encouragement for a new life respect if you lack in this area.

Sorry for any repeated text, although they are important messages that have now doubly sank in to your mind. I have been up to my ears in lack of order, comprehension and memory does not allow recognition of recognition of repeats.

BOOK2 Orignal; drunk drive deterrent

Contents;

1- Boredom mounts advantage takers take - vulnerability and isolation.
2- Disability and drink - assumptions from a 'knowing' society.

3- Dont do this dont do that - Discrimination secrets revealed.

4- Emotions rule - experiments, self driving cars. ethics, emotions, disability acceptance.

5- establish sense - Avoidance.

6- Facades deduce - Good intention, jealousy, false fronts, ignorance, childhood.

7- Follow your purpose - Differing forms of people.

8- Memories from my past - Is this really mental health?

9- Mum- Brief my story.

10- Psychology - Realities, beliefs, Zen.

11- The mystical - Spirituality and deceit, because I thought.

12- Still have a brain - Lost my mind in rehab!

13- Summer - Crazy days, early awareness in hospital.

14- Susan - Unintended judgements, companionship, judgement, a death.

15- The door is wide - A new inception of disability exclusion and inclusion.

16- Intention; - A best society

17- Dont die a fool. The lessons are long and difficult or sudden and devastating.

18- An abrupt close

1- Boredom mounts advantage takers take - vulnerability and isolation.

A quiet experience can result in a person becoming more vulnerable, you will do anything for collaboration with peers, just conversation as your struggles with walking mean you do not go out much or you have spent all your money partly on entertaining the advantages and sure enough boredom sets in.

Trying to inspire yourself is made difficult with expectation of the serene except this serenity has murky skies. There is not much beauty in solitude, unless you are that way inclined, I am not this at all. Actually like everything this depends on how you view this time. Some will only love a quiet moment, radio on doing what they choose, these are mostly people with careers or other lifetime fillers, family, friends, business etcetera.

I choose to write, I am not one for chores or other entertainments, writing is a beautiful past time, the hours stream past and I get an adrenalin reward after writing a good piece. I feel I am of service because all my writing has a moral backing with reason. I talk a lot of my experiences but these have mainly only appeared because of my lack of sense. I was too content to plod on when most things were good so was shown, if I was not going to search for this extra to existence then I was to be shown another reality. One that I always felt immune from and denied appreciation of.

Do not take life or you ability for granted, you want to know why drunk driving and disability equality are such seriously taken topics? Or why mental health is somewhat a taboo issue, you can fully regard these from the place in the same direction as ignorance.

Your vulnerability will teach you much but in that position you have no stature to argue with a listened to voice. They say do not have regrets, this is very difficult when your own stupidity lands you in isolated matrimony. Look to the future is more advice, I am trying and only recently really envisage better things because there is some life style decisions on the horizon, but this is not possible when, as millions of people are entrapped in loneliness and isolation.

2- Disability and drink - assumptions from a 'knowing' society.

A wish to rectify the relationship between, and non judgemental acceptance, the able to the disabled. Talking to those who are not aware, do you realize how patronizing it is to refer to a disability first off and say 'your so strong, you've been through much' when they don't even know you, or to remark when someone in a wheelchair says I am just going to run to the shop. Common vocabulary is still used, everyday speech is hard to diverge but it seems this is shouting for listeners. An example of why your wrong if you do this exact example, my friend that had a severe disability, who joined an athletics club and was encouraged to, in a fashion jog, even attempt to jump small hurdles! So, you know the saying, judge, book, cover, don't.

Disability is not to be pitied, that is like pitying a child who stumbles, you just don't, you get them up, brush them off and give them some love and they are bouncing on their way.

These people are some of the most resilient people you will meet but often we aren't given the time to get to know this. Disability faces obstacles the majority of you 'normal' folk won't even have nightmares about. True grit is required not to become isolated and venture into society. People think a commute to work can be stressful, how about thinking of every obstacle and all the barriers along with the looks from others, the kids remarks to Mum or

Dad, not getting served in pubs because your assumed drunk, people going over roads because they dare not walk near the drunk or they are disillusioned by disability.

These people have a deeply seated fear, perhaps unconsciously because they sense a threat of they're own mortality, do not want 'that' in their own life so immediately don't relate. Or think that the disabled individual cannot master the simplest task, I have witnessed a blind man waiting for the beep at lights to go over a main road, on his own, no dog no stick, and another blind man, this time with a dog being extremely social in a pub enjoying himself. Now why can that not be comprehended by a majority?

Physical disability does not mean, because we look like we can't walk properly that we are stupid or can't manage. Take for granted some of us can and do, the rest of us have our own barriers to combat that is often taken as the cripple moaning but more likely totally out of your realm of appreciation.

I thought I was somewhat good at portraying my trials, my ego takes over when I consider myself as opposed to ignorance as an expert in minority ordeals, but I listened to an audio, Disability studies, by Colin Cameron. Their are people studying what I have been writing about in a less eloquent manner, and that have the articulacy to demonstrate efficiently. There are many experts out there, it makes little sense why disabled people are disregarded so much and even less sense why drink driving is still an issue. Thats what got me here, some people whether knowing or not sense the distaste of disability but will still drive drunk! The saying, the simplest things can reap the biggest rewards is the same as the easiest things can cause the most havoc. Drink driving is easy, easy done, are you easy? Do you want to be done? Done in?

My mother was getting out her car one day, she wobbled and stumbled a little, a passer gave her such a look of disgrace assuming she was drunk and getting out of a car had been drunk driving. Mum being as witty as she is just thought, go on say something and I will make you look this big. She did not say anything so Mum with her amazing temperance just kept quiet.

She has a Menieres disease which causes dizziness and effects her balance, that is all, she was not drinking. I commented it is good that you can have the confidence in a heated situation to have that intention and to not cause an uproar when things did not need words. A disabled person may not have this confidence or ability to remain calm and think of apt ways to effectively articulate, brain injury for example can cause word finding difficulties made worse when emotions rise.

 I am telling the stories of disability for a double purpose, to help all those drinkers really think about not driving, they can accept not wanting these words to include themselves and to improve acceptance and equal treatment for disabled people.

I have done this myself so know what struggle we have, I referred to non-disabled people as able, disabled are just as able in certain areas. This can be regarded as discrimination on my part, wholly unintentional but disabled people or activists may take offence to this speech. I comprehend what an uphill struggle disability equality is as myself has succumbed to some of the things I and others speak of. Discrimination can be unintended but just as harmful. I don't propose this intending total innocence.

When I spoke of language being misconstrued such as a disabled person running to the shop or I talk of or I hear you, there are many examples. I have mistakenly done this exact thing with a disabled friend whom is the final person I want to offend.

The stories of disability; Not much I will admit but I have done some research and the stories of disabled people were just like mine, hard to comprehend but true. This is happening so much and needs to stop. Mum listened to a very small part of an audio I bought about disability, she thought I had written it in part because she recognised so many of the 'tales' told. This is happening all about the world, the same or similar things, we need to believe when a story is repetitively told, disabled voices should be heard.

Memory can be recalled even though you may not recall the original justification, knowledge can be mistaken because of this. If information is delivered incorrectly you go about assuming this is true but your knowledge was wrong from the start.

3- Dont do this dont do that - Discrimination secrets revealed.

Don't do this, don't do that, drink driving is one discrimination is another. Just some out of the endless advice on do's and don't, so this is easily comprehensible that certain people choose to ignore advice or rules and practice the exact thing deterred. Comprehend this, that there are mystical essences influencing every area of our lives, so if you are secretly at something you should not, get real this is no secret and will have an affect in some form.

Dents or scratches on cars, this is where I started. Blissful I carried on, or possibly you are pulled over and breathalysed, perhaps you getaway with this, I did, blissful I carried on. Or perhaps you go to court, are sentenced, loose your license, your job, your livelihood, your social life and your respect. Or possibly, you have little choice if you are breaking the rules remember, these essences control much in your existence and you have a minor crash, this happened to me, blissful and pissed I carried on. Or quite likely you have a more serious crash, someone is hurt, so you loose all the above... and go to jail. Or just as likely, you cripple yourself, lose all the above, get charged some of the above, if you are well enough and have to start relearning simple life sequences, retraining your mind and skills, all is lost from the brain-damage. Perhaps you can walk, perhaps not, perhaps you can talk, perhaps not. Perhaps you wish you had died in the crash, theres nothing left to live for, perhaps you are strong and face your new life...

...Or quite probably, you smash your head open, sense your partner fly through the windscreen, then yourself die!

Do we need to tempt fate? Do we need lessons? Do I need to spell out? This rule is for you and your friends own good. Drink and drive if ya so determined your not happy with how life is, I guarantee this will be one of your biggest regrets and you will be less happy with your new life.

How ya getting home? Like where ya live do ya? Oh is it miles from town? Drink drivings alright then! No honestly, go on, try why dont ya?

Me I was all left, because it was my right side that was injured, and all the relationships that meant anything to me, and my gratitude, and the rest of my life, and manoeuvring obstacles and in society. Think your accepted, don't cause issues because when your alone in all your splendid isolation, doing nowt but consolation, you might get a little bored. Ya social animal!

4- Emotions rule - experiments, self driving cars. ethics, emotions, disability acceptance.

Emotions rule: Machines are said not to be able to make decisions based on ethics, neither can humans in a hurry or emotional moment.

Ever hear about the samaritans rushing to the lecture hall? Experimenters placed a poorly dressed man in obvious discomfort on their path. How many ethics or morals are misplaced? How many good Samaritans rushed by? How many other religious or otherwise folk dispel their teaching in times of need? Apparent or not.

None of these good people stopped to offer help, that is not to say they are not good people, most people with an agender on their mind will defer what they live by to attain that agender.

Back to technology, the self driving car, will, I only think swerve into oncoming traffic rather than hit a child. This can be said to be ethical but I suspect the car would do this as opposed to hit any obstacle.

Ethics and morals play, or rather underplay a huge part in the lives of those socially hardened people with disabilities. Religious or not, men and women are sometimes inclined to turn the other cheek, just figure the percentage of the average citizen that defy expectation.

New rules are made after disability is introduced to much of society. Programmer or political bias can influence liberty in man and machine but would you rather be in the reactive car driven by a machine or a drunk teenager?

The emotions of the persons with a disability, are somewhat nulled somewhat heightened. We know from personal experience to ignore a lot of what goes on everyday even when accompanying onlookers say did you did not notice that did you, probably best. Or we can rise to extreme anger at the smallest injunction because they are so ridiculous and tedious that we have just had enough. Even this those of us will toughen up to but tempers can flare at seeming insignificances. Those with a mind intact and senses to enable will tolerate and show temperance and wit in their response or lack of, but as most of disability is assumed there are those not able to, maybe. I suspect in their own way, socially acceptable and warranted or not cope and deal with these situations in their own ways.

We think in groups, things, social aptitudes are developed in groups. No one person is responsible for the alienation of disability, this has em merged through centuries and only in the latter has disability acceptance gained ground.

Policies and movements are made in groups, there is a large group of people opposing the inbuilt regimes that people with impairments face but just as this has taken years to evolve this has taken generations to start change in other minds.

There is still the conflict of right and wrong in self-judgement, what I propose by this is that some people are inclined to do the right thing some the wrong thing not because they are choosing individuality but because they are caught up in group think. There are many pioneers who have this individuality choice presupposed and this is becoming prominent, my promising outlook infers.

I learn bits, I sense a lot but I have not studied many academic areas so take my writing how you will, as a personal memoir to learn by I am hoping. My writing style has evolved much so do not be surprised if you witness something you disagree with or is not entirely correct. My purpose is apparent, to decline drink/drug driving and to enhance disability equality and inclusion. I want to cause debate amongst all people and education is a priority.

5- establish sense - Avoidance.

Establish sense, even in your thought, misapprehended speech can result in detrimental consequence. All the things I suggest are the faults of my life, I have experience of all I talk about, I am not a professor but trust me I wish I did not but I do know. You can avoid this and lead a productive life when you listen to these.

A few people, professional or friend are against me because of my mistaken past. Know where you are going and what path you are on if you have not yet decided.

6- Facades deduce - Good intention, jealousy, false fronts, ignorance, childhood.

All the good intention I have and there is still jealousy and false fronts. They are never gonna keep me down! I ascertain victory over all obstacle trying to hinder such a good cause. My suggestion and speech has made this hindrance more apparent, do not think you cannot control your existence because this is one of the main learnings in life.

As a child you vulnerable, susceptible and at the mercy of your caregivers but as you mature and once, however finally you appreciate this sentiment thus will a new life emerge.

Think that control of your environment is feasible because this is the truest statement, all speech, thought intention and ignorance will deliver. Rules wavered and diligence ignored will head you for difficulty even as you found life easy or not. The rewards will produce much more for you if you take the narrow difficult path, broad is the gate that many find and walk, easy is this way. Challenges and character building are hard to find, you may say that you would rather not have challenges in your way but this leads to a simple non-productive life and no character encapsulation.

If you would dare just ignore the teaching and regulations and find a truly obnoxious path to try and follow. I will be the first to admit, I know this very well because in part I did this resulting in catastrophic implication that is near impossible to navigate but not un explorable.

7- Follow your purpose - Differing forms of people.
follow your purpose, follow your heart no matter what. Things will grow good. Material objects can have meaning, they can matter but dont let this sway without reason. If no one believes in you but you've always had, just a feeling then believe in yourself and follow this feeling. People arrive in forms, form one are good advisors, honest truthful advisors, these are worth recognizing and listening to. Form two however are to be mistrusted they are either

misled or devious, or possibly absolutely naive through no fault of their own. No matter who from you learn the treachery against you as one grows, am not talking down to or degrading anyone just this is fact. As is the good deeds done to you, you will greatly regard these more.

No matter the teaching I was dealt I was one of those totally naive individuals who could not be swayed, because of my prowess or abilities I denied all except those abilities were outweighed by stubborn naivety and prowess was egotistical to little life knowledge actually. I knew what I enjoyed, how to make people laugh and my then current wants but I did not know the meaning of life or how to sustain a healthy world view and other vicissitudes.

Ignorance will lead to your own destruction, when I heard words akin to this I blissfully waned them off as mature people thinking they know my life better than I do, well possibly or possibly not your life but certainly overall existence. You want to exist? Then recognize all words and actions and single out those you adamantly listen to, you will decipher the wrong from the right.

Because I relied on my magnificent colourful imagination that I thought was a mind needing no input I veered off path, got into trouble including drugs, fights and drunk driving. I was to be taught by life nearly ending and forever changed then on. You want to really learn, learn now or carry on the path of self destruction and face having no choice but to acclimatize an all altered existence, or die.

Myself I find it hard to in the past imagine me saying all I say but I cannot believe how I have matured in my growing years and since a life changing incident.

As you learn of things that you dont regard, have no current meaning for you or seem by the wayside you will later recall these lessons, be this not too late. Catastrophe is what it has taken for me to finally alter my ways and really learn to be an adult, this has taken years and years of avoidable adjustments and living the consequences for what seems all my life.

I dream of training those who require to be taught and I will teach those who just havent had the chance or are self obsessed like I was or are too young to realise. You if honest quite possibly fit into one of these very broad categories or can honesty foretelling, realize another.

We can make a better place and this starts with each one of you. There was a beginning for me, all the obstacles on the journey I am still overcoming, life is the best medicine but also the biggest obstacle.

One can say dont let people divert you from your path, not always possible I say, people protect and defend and a mind in one of these modes can influence and just as easily be influenced. Your instinct can find your way back to the right path.

Learn and listen to yourself as well as good advice. Decline following the path of no moral or juvenile behaviour, any age group can do this even I am starting here.

I realize this all can be seen as common sense, but lives differ, abuse, suffering or other facets can dictate a moral upbringing. As I sense things the population still has a lot of issues that are helped with even uncommon common sense to really make this an in the majority topic.

Dont take offence just let all be taught to the immature and do your bit in evolution.

8- Memories from my past - Is this really mental health?

The memories from my past are haunting, how can I continue with thoughts that are regarded as bad mental health to others. I have so much beneficial work to bring, perhaps yes I just need to be patient but this is hard, I am at my wits end, with occurrence justifying - All is made difficult, but I have acknowledged in the past and wrote that the difficulty on a path will lead to more satisfaction when overcome, this is therefore going to be one rewarding journey.

I have been as honest as my life allows, I am leaning towards more secrecy but my words have been blunt and to the point to have an impact. I am trying to deter catastrophes (drink driving and disability denials) but I learn through my writing and experience that I have much worth teaching others. Now I cannot be sure what world I live in but I know there are issues with families, society, self-esteem and that there are still drink drivers. This is enough to say that I should continue and the promised rewards intend I shall continue despite the knock backs and refusals, Whatever I am so eagerly awaiting will come to truth very soon I can feel.

I am not yet enlightened despite what people may or may not think, I am, I put down to my upbringing but I think there is something else involved. I am however extremely astute to emotions in others and bodily feeling/senses in myself. This can and will take me further but until then there are other influences and effectors that are near impossible to exempt from such a dull life. Don't get me wrong I enjoy my work, can sense others benefit but need proof. Either statistics or email or in some other fashion.

The super-natural, regarding my foundations has been taking form and to a lost mind is still hard to apprehend but people get used to anything and my familiarity is not justifying.

My writing is a lot from self knowledge but do I really know? I can express my thoughts when writing I will archive this in personal speech even holding myself when emotions rise. I once before mediation (again, is that even a word?), had these skills, I was as apt as many at articulating and expressing the smallest most difficult to verbalise statures. This is returning, and will definitely fill me with the upmost joy when it facilitates my wants for these causes.

Destination unknown but i just know that great things await me and my work.

I had life so easy and rewarding when was younger, I remember having the thought, it came true! That I would suffer as much as what I witnessed and not be so credited with a happy life, not to say I didn't have issues when young,I did. I was so empathetic that I seriously used to imagine living lives of the less fortunate existences I viewed.

You know what they say,imagination is the master key to all, be careful what you imagine, I am not worried though because I also distinctly imagined the miraculous which is yet to emerge fully

9- Mum- Brief my story.

My heightened awareness, in dubious areas leads to me actually realizing myself a bit more. I am still some of the time egotistical, do not know how or why because I really feel a failure in other places.

My writing demonstrates, to me anyway, irregular

inconsistencies of which I am not proud of. In my last book I consoled Mum without explanation, I degraded her very much for which I expose this; Mum is and has been for years my very best friend, I cannot judge any parenting because I am not a parent.

We had multiple difficulties of which she dealt with astonishing efficiency, I however kept up stress levels in all of us and did not regard as much as I should have until recent years. You can say that that is all part of growing up but I am middle aged! A big trauma delayed this acknowledgement but also enhances this because of what she went through to remain by my side.

I have had masterful upheaval in the latter part of my life, average upheaval throughout my teens and so so stresses when young, ain't we all so what is so special about my life. The Mystical has built my entire life because I have purpose realised now.

| always had the thoughts and feelings that life was going to be good, I would do amazing things, the reason I am in debt is because I often thought I had found the answer, being multiple of them. What almost killed me was my saviour, the answer was there all along. If you find me hard to believe take a look at drinkdrivedeterrent mind travels amid purpose revealed by JD.R. You will never think in the same way about much.

I was slightly, ever so a bit much too honest, my publisher edited lots, I still propose truth but withhold the unessential. There are those that will get me and, I am hoping those that will not, just take this as unnecessary information.

I have started this my second book before the first is published and I am still not entirely sure what the main content will consist of.

Head-injury was just my thought, I have personal societal and familiar al experience of this resulting from drunk driving, take a look at my previous book if you want to forever determine yours or someone else appreciation. Drunk drive deterrent Mind travels amid purpose revealed by JD.R
I start from the very first time I drank and drove. I know very well that memory is affected by brain-damage but I can recall the thoughts I had and the feeling of making it home, oh this ain't so bad I can do this again. I was petrified at first, driving at way under the speed limit then I thought I had better speed up because I might look suspicious. Then before I knew it I was driving at excessive speeds the alcohol soon forgets first cautions.
My so called friends, I did not have many or long established ones, used to tell me to slow down, not one of them although they were in my car said you shouldn't drink drive its stupid. Not wanting to face their own vulnerability at getting in the car and don't think because I was speeding was the main reason I crashed, there was something in the road, this could happen to anyone.
I really don't know what a different mess I would be if I caused the passenger a head-injury resulting in disability and years of recovery.
That gives me another suggestion that was partly covered in my other book, I want to promote disability acceptance and inclusion so will no doubt talk about this, this is a work in progress but Divinity has got me this far so hold out for the best.

I sit here in all my seclusion desperately wanting to assist the world and I can I will if you are looking or listening at this. Where was I? Drunk-driving in the early days, if you have a minor skid or bump take this as a sign. I had many and never did take what was trying so hard to tell me, do not assume though you will not crash and potentially cripple yourself or kill your girlfriend or boyfriend on the very first drunken excursion.

I was even stopped by police after drinking earlier in the day and breathalysed, I was just under the limit, he says from what you have told us and your reading you are very lucky, this does not happen often, take it a sign. Less than a month later I was in a-coma due to drunk driving!

I have a promised purpose, this is to help you all to not difficult sense, I saw the adverts, although I am pleased to say they are much more hard hitting now and I viewed the posters. We need something else, I used to give talks on these subjects and know, very proudly that I have stopped teenagers to hardened drink drivers from practising this absolute ridicule. If you want to check my story, disability is very easily apprehended, perhaps your mates won't even be around for that! I will stop any from being so naive.

Drink driving KILLS, is not a fanciful slogan this is more than the truth, if not physically this will kill your personality, your emotions, your entire livelihood, work, family and other relations the lot.

As a skint uneducated teen I was chuffed at saving twenty quid on a taxi home, now I would gladly have paid the last of my money as opposed to the twenty years since attempting to drive drunk.

Early days.

I cannot remember a thing of intensive care, what others

tell me I did some embarrassing things, too embarrassing to mention. I woke in an animated place, did not think my Mum was really who she said and thought I was being witty outdoing all these sci-fi nurses and doctors. I was not outdoing them just another patient to them.

Disability.

You will have trouble getting in cars getting off and manoeuvring on buses or trains, walking saying you can still walk, on gravel or grass or ice or steps and uneven ground.

Brain-damage.

Full stop. You will have trouble with everything from getting on with those you love to filling our forms to being accepted the same from mates to getting even partly accepted by many in society as what you think you are still worth to accepting your own blasted denials.

10- Psychology - Realities, beliefs, Zen.

this is a cause and effect reality, my misguided belief system is wrong. i dont fully believe in spirituality after all, not the kind i thought i knew, well dont agree with is a better way of saying. i believe only i make my reality.

perceived pleasure< or pain>

this is virtual reality, we act on perceptions and misperceptions, no difference between illusion and reality.

how do you create your world

this is such a great course i am two inches taller and significantly better looking.

thoughts and feelings are always interrelated, watch your thoughts match your feelings

the most misconstrued thought is outside causes feeling

when it is my thought, i cause happiness or the opposite by my stream of thought

feelings are simple, drama is what creates the story, remove the story and the feelings are simple

we are sum of our history, 80% personality formed between 0-7yearsold, imprint period/ more like 80-95% values/beliefs are programmed. kids do not discriminate. they need good life advice.

dont read/look at or listen to crap.

born to succeed programmed to fail.

Depregramme yourself, programmes/values/beliefs, money, family, honesty, hardwork, trust, honour/ego, nature of man, what you deserve,politics, religion, fairness, truth, success, respect.

zen, drill the truth, 99.97% isnt true

much of what we believe is in conflict

thoughts create feelings create actions

we are what we think, our thought creates our world

everything i am experiencing is a reflection of self, be the change you want to see the world, your view of the world changes when you change

believing something does not make true, believe something true but its illusion

99% of what we believe is not true. different levels of understanding leads to different reality

believe something, never check if true=dillusion

confirmation bias we block anything that doesnt support our belief system, dont let ego get in way, dont let lies lead way

find ultimate truth

reality therapy

3 illusions, we think we know other people, we think we

know ourselves, we think we understand the world
-we know what other people tell us -we see through our biases -we often see what other people want us to, -we distort with our history, -we distort with our belief system -we distort with our self esteem, -miscommunication, -false associations
-we believe what other people tell us, we see through our biases, -we often see what others want us to, -we distort with our history, -we distort with our belief systems, we distort with our self esteem, -we cant see ourselves, - we hide/distort our pain
-"   " we makes serious logic errors, -we are a sample of one
ego a false sense of self created by unconscious identification with the mind.
proximity rule, avoidance can be beautiful.

rational emotive behavioural therapy.
sane be good to yourself, emotional, change behaviour, you dont have to be sick to get better
we think, we believe, action
a activating event, b belief, c consequence d dispute
disturbing event-feeling-action >yell >thought -self talk-rules >mad-bop
is the meaning you give the event
thought-feeling response always match. what am i feeling??
change stream of thought. like to think??
think? < mad (self talk) focus on belief
 how can i look at this in the positive. quality of input is quality of output
reduce negative self talk
belief systems, idea/story made up

have decided, with assistance, what i believe and what i create. i let go of past pain, guilt and regret. i learn from my past to make a better future in the now. contribution, getting the most out of life, do no harm. how can i contribute more.

remove old pain old suffering, false self, story, belief system, removal of illusions
strugglc creates counter force, evey time someone pushes, pull when they pull push
you are not intelligent if, or gonna expand your awareness when you are intoxicating yourself with cigarettes and alcohol, thats a form of denial

zen.
more open i am, more i receive,
each day like a student at their first class, i prepare my mind like a blank slate for the day to write upon.
three levels of understanding, i hear and i forget, i see and i remember, i do and i understand.
wisdom, taking everything in without filter, the philosophy of zen is about finding truth.
zen is about being completely alive, search for truth, de condition ourselves, enlightenment, serenity.
multiple levels of understanding, see the layer between things.
completely alive, connectedness, present, aware, blank slate, absorbing, enjoyment, contentment.
to lighten, no mind, let go of ego, be in now, seek wisdom

within without, release.

search for truth, not mine not yours ultimate reality, useful, multiple truths, application.

how we recondition ourselves.

layers, layered truth, extra sensory awareness, new understanding.

live now, only time there is never trade now for later, past future illusion.

5 roots of suffering, not knowing whats real, grasping and clinging to the unreal, being afraid of the unreal and recoiling, identifying with imaginary self, fear of death.

all problems are maintained. the mind is a machine, designed to make meaning out of everything, the brain is a dumb goal seeking mechanism.

our responses are not a reaction to reality they are preprogrammed responses to belief system... but thats just a story.

Identify strengthen, observe weaken ego.

Neurotic repetitive thought, stop, right lets go on to the solution.

Inside your mind you are the prisoner, jailer and hero. solve your own mental problem.

Learn to dis identify with mind. who covered your eye, why did ya keep this covered.

11- The mystical - Spirituality and deceit, because I thought.

spirituality is amazingly deceitful, i am either in a spiritual world or i am not, you cant effect me with your rules when you declined me. dont give me thought then blame me, dont scare me with other people and your mystical ways, make things good then make them bad and everyone thinks i am enlightened because of realising some things that i am given.

either enlighten me and keep out or fucking do one.

i have been told things my whole life, that were meaningless so i forgot them, by spiritually inclined people on the street, i am given all these statements, later than necessary to act on, as thought when they are messages from the divine. they come as thought because of my wrong programming of events. well if you are going to treat a human as spiritual you can allow for mistakes.

dont keep secrets from those you call spiritual, dont keeps secrets from yourself, you havent a clue of the entire story, i am never supposed to behave like this but you effected me so i do. i would rather you projected me back to my usual life upbringing and mine life and stayed away with your hopes of what you knew had a slim chance of occurring. remember i have been spoken incomprehensible words my whole life so i know someone knew, only God knows the truth and God will save me.

spiritual indeed, i cannot write a bigger misdemeanour.

spiritual people in the street, in the supermarket treat me funny because they 'know' they know better, well i am telling ya, they dont.

another thing, if spiritual people are going to have everyday commonly used words as their names dont be mistaken that they are being spoken about because these words arise in nearly every sentence, i thought a spiritual place was advanced, yeah i am human talking from human perspectives but dont try and half include any you seclude, prior programming errors or not. i only know, think i know, pretty sure i know because of these words spoken my whole life, that are reminded by divine message and the reaction i get. your world need a lot of sorting too before this can truly be regarded as superior.

i am telling ya, there is no such thing as wholly,truly spiritual, yes i am talking to each one of you who thinks or thinks they know they are spiritual. come from my existence then try to find an argument. deviousness and deceit are not spiritually describing words and that i have encountered all along this path.

Oh thoughts get listened to, do they so and acted on, well why not my actions considering that is what humans are taught, most of humanity anyway, except for those exceptionally lucky minority that had parenting in the know.

I was taught this does not matter what ya think, ya cannot control your thought, this all depends on what action ya take.

I do not mean to talk in slang but this is all enveloped from spiritual emphasis having influence.

Because they thought, they chose and because this was wrong my life suffers. Because they fear they have done wrong, they affect my thought, my life to detriments that expose. They take so I expose.

They did this to a fine brain then listened to all the thought produced by an inhibited brain, I no longer have a mind, you find our why in my other books, all I say here this was enabled by them.

My totally abstract thought came to light and now all people are the same, minus the minority lucky few billion who are my neighbours and soon to become friends. Ya have a human feeling sorry for the awakened, yeah residing in human only category of existence. Missing the true deed am I? You're missing the true picture of my time.

Why affect others to inform when just leads to paranoia, mistaken ordeals and the rest. Yeah so I did not complete every demand, what goes for me goes for every awakened person, why no? That said I am refused by yourselves, that is right not fully awakened so I am exempt from this consideration.

Why give me power beyond your control or at least choice, if ya knew how things would go? But oh, ya suddenly have choice when this goes how ya not like, well I do not like either and this was all instigated by yourselves!

Synchronicities are an outweighed area, what is the reason? Because my overwhelmed brain said so, well if I can own that power, you are taking nothing from me and I promote all and every productive word I ever spoke and thought. Think ya can break rules just because ya made them, what goes for one goes for all, I remake and write my own productions.

I make my life, my protection what I always knew this would be. I am the god of my life, me not mistaken thought or impeded upheaval.

12- Still have a brain - Lost my mind in rehab!

Break a bad habit, I have many I wish to subdue, noted today that the method I only started less than a week ago really works. I had enough of easy daily nourishment. So I visualized myself in the vicinity of acquiring this and rehearsed denying that, refusing this when offered, I succeeded quite easily and bought something of more nutritional value.

Start with this story because I want to emphasize how routine ingrained norms in the brain are easily navigated. Dont get me wrong I have much to work on but am trying even the un recommended or less popular avenues of overbearing these.

but there is a lot more to life than just accepting or battling with your mind. spiritual laws, how can laws govern the uninitiated, the misled, the tricked or misguided for responsible or not reason?

 rehabilitation centres are full of trickery, this is a description; it is their jobs to trick clients into recovery. this works, this worked for me but because i was nearly a chosen for one big mission and my future endeavour was foreseen by the awakened, i was fooled in allsorts of angles and totally disregarded.

jealousy has haunted my time, i without much explanation will just say, a top neuro psychologist may have been jealous of an injured clients mind. he practised defence against psychic exploitation, i often saw him with gaping jaw at intricacies i know werent part of the schedule. i was that much in tune, astute, empathetic and humorous, i was proud of myself even before my rebirth at rehab! since my mind was taken and other effecting significant powers, i have had very muddled thought, loss of confidence and lack of belief in myself, so i searched and searched and i am locating possible ways out.

my childhood made me extremely emotionally sensitive outwardly, i am still astute, the small things are sensed, others think i am mind reading, i am not. i missed my chance at awakening once, i follow a similar path to my prior destiny in doing my best as a mere human to achieve mastery i never comprehended i was on the path to.

mere human influenced by spiritual forces, things i eat, thing i drink, think, physically do, thing i say and write. ok so some of these if they were fully regarded soon enough, can be rewarding but what i physically do prevents awareness until an episode has near past some of the time. the stuff i eat and drink effects my thought, i am told to stop eating! STOP f**king eating, if you are going to raise a mere child without added lessons or knowing, like the Buddha had, then ya cannot suppose he will ignore his inbuilt childhood lessons, ya need to eat! dont try and tell me for the first time a quarter way through my life, potentially, to stop eating.

though i have bent these laws to suit my now limited existence, what i say productively goes that way, i have repaired the past, my thoughts and all, made my future magnificent and a shining light effective and changed my destiny, after all, absolutely anything is possible in spiritual realms. so my life is not what this was designed as but will remain just as effecting and enhancing and enjoyable.

i have struggled, against friends, family, my own mind, whats left of this but i still witness the end of the tunnel. family have given up on me,professionals dont always know whats best, except those that know. one of them, she is a social worker called lisa, now she is a hero. you might not be aware of the lingo i use yet, hero/enemy from someone helping you home to someone bumping into ya, and every facet in between, above and below, these i learned to regard as either hero or enemy, i dont intend superman or war, just figure of speech.

so ya never do know the path that will unfold, less thou are born awakened, as some are. a path of treachery can lead to a life of bliss and vice versa. i am going to utilise what i have learned for my anti drunk drive message.

ya think you have done wrong, ya have regrets, then you are given a mission. you dont adhere to all the faculties so treachery, turned bliss changes back to treachery. thought this was difficult when ya did not have a clue did ya? crawl out this hole ya appear to reside in, then watch people making all the mistakes you made without saying anything or trying to warn them. good luck.

13- Summer - Crazy days, early awareness in hospital.
The summer was great, days fishing, playing football or in the local pub until late. I passed my driving test that summer, this was after lonely relocation, had couple of good mates later on but used to spend a lot of time with early teens, I was 18, they were just boys.
This is the story of a regarded as unfair, difficult life leading to lack of regard which eventually effected the rest of my life.
What a present, for my birthday my Grandparents paid for a motor, finally I could get more independence. It was a warm night, I had two very young adolescents in my car. An average looking 1litre Metro, I was proud of this but it was tediously slow even with pedal to the metal.
It was a dark night, we pulled up down a back lane for a

crafty joint.

On the way back out I was seeing double, didn't adjust my driving, in fact I was belting along, in my tediously slow 1litre, round the corner except I didn't make this bend, I crashed into the bushes sliding up an embankment.

So stoned We weren't phased, got out made some adjustments to the knackered undercarriage of my car and went zooming off again. If the tree was closer and bushes did not slow us this would have been catastrophic I am in no doubt.

Very late to mature I was acting younger than these two boys.

In another town, I was on my own, we had moved to the country, my life was very quiet I was often out by myself with nothing to do no where to go. I would park right under the cameras and head for a solemn drink in a pub or club.

Drank shots back then, I would come to my car legless and no questions ask, I was driving home, cannot afford a taxi, £20 was more than my life was worth!

Pelting in a thirty limit I misjudged the bend again. There was quite a drop to the path beneath.

The only thing stopping me from smashing down into a lowered walkway was a metal guardrail, dented this very badly, mounted the curb and punctured a tyre.

I was reckless indeed but refused to take heed of what these incidents were telling me. In fact a fresh recollection, I had taken heed in as much as I was not speeding on this road. The near misses had scared me I was slowing down to beneath the speed limit but I was still drunk, you will crash at any speed don't think because you are going within the limit that you are safe.

You might not think you drive recklessly but equally the double vision from whatever the intoxicant and two feet to the side and you are head on with that tree or you miss the railing and plunge ten feet into the shopfront.

Take all warnings, minor and major as somebody watching over you and granting a second, third, fourth, fiftieth chance!

They say those caught drunk driving have practised this something like sixty times before arrest or are you caught out? No matter how adept you think you are at handling the road you can be caught out on you one hundredth drunken excursion, and crash and kill and die. If you live good chances are one life has died and you are starting surrealism from here because you will not be the same person, will not think the same, walk the same if at all, talk the same or relate in your old way.

I had a new job in a new town, fresh start you might say, but no. We had been playing pool drinking all afternoon in the pub where all my new friends lived.

I lived down a dual carriageway, went onto this and immediately there was flashing lights behind me, I slowed to let them past but they stayed behind, eventually I pulled over.

The policeman said you were a bit all over as you came onto the main road,have you been drinking?

Oh no this was it, I really done it now, job, friends and social life all gone, though I did not appreciate this at the time, I calmly said yes but that was hours ago, I told a fib as to how much I had drank, he proceeded to breathalyse me.

First beep recognises alcohol on your breath second beep

is the decider that your over the limit.

So I had no qualms when came the initial beep but waited for the longest few seconds of my life, it never made another sound.

Wow your just under, I can tell you've had more than you say, this doesn't happen often, take this as a sign. Relieved but not truly acknowledged, my move to the country would have been over without my car.

Blazaay I drove home.

Less than a month later we were going clubbing, remember laughing with all my mates.

Today I used to go to the club by myself and sit pitiful watching the dance floor.

Anyway we came outside all merry, got in the car...

Then I woke in a dream, science fiction had taken over, people acting like doctors and nurses think I cannot suss out that the matrix is taken over and nothing or no one is real.

Whats the deal they reckon I was drunk driving but I had stopped that foolish game, I can remember slowing right down.

My friends were now all in wheelchairs or bedridden, I used to choke at dinner time, so called nurses come into the toilet and wipe my ass for me. Surreal ain't the phrase , surrealism times infinity!

I was content making patterns on the ceiling with my gaze then an angel walked in! NO, NO, NO.

This is really happening. I used to work with her.

I still did not catch on, I told her the abstract truth, that Mum wasn't really who she said, all these people think they are fooling me, I have had enough of this film I want to go home. Was out last night can remember conversation.

It had been three months in intensive care, in a-coma.

Then I said I am going to escape and call my real Mum, she will not believe this.

Skidded, hit the curb, put my head through the window, take out parked cars and a brick wall.

This was enough, fate had had enough of me not listening, this was serious.

What if we'd gone in the river and drowned? My mate accompanied me with cuts and bruises in the ambulance, he had to watch me lose consciousness. The signs were not good.

14- Susan - Unintended judgements, companionship, judgement, a death.

Unintended judgements are very apparent and most are susceptible to this. Example; did you see the looks on the judges faces when Susan Boyle walked out on Britains Got Talent? She had not even said anything and there were disgusting looks of immediate denials. This is a totally different scenario but alike occurrence to Disability except this lady probably did not get these looks in all situations, every street she walked up and every encounter she made.

I get that she was not the usual attendee but book, cover, don't comes to mind again. I guess the same can be assumed if an overweight footballer walked on the pitch but I once knew a particularly stocky lad who could sprint as fast and have a very strong kick about.

Companionship; even acquainting possible friends is difficult for Disabled people, they each have their own assumptions and some are hard let go of no matter the proof or will be wrongly reinforced.

We cannot, I know even I believe in acquainting twin soul mates who you just feel a connection with but we all of us should not judge on first even second or third appearance. Judgements should be held back I believe until you can say, oh I am not going to say but this is a prolonged time if ever, certainly relationships years in the making.

Knew of one girl who always demonstrated self-control when this choosing a partner showed and though she had some self-esteem issues was very deliberate when she came to giving of herself emotionally and physically. I think life got on top of her though as she met one man later in life, who turned out to be a cunning and devious man, he had judged her where he wanted her to be and she placed wrongful judgement on him to embody the correct choice for a life partner and they were married within two months of acquainting. Needless to say this led to miserable expensive times for her when she put on weight, was living unhealthily and back then looked to have added years to her age. I am pleased to say within the same timescale of acquaintance to marriage the divorce proved a best move, now she looks twenty years younger, lost much weight and has started to smile again

Disability, whether unintended or not, devious or innocent is judged. I have been judged because of how I used to talk, walk, think and behave but I as many do, have proven Disability does not have to be ever enduring and will affect different people differently at various stages of life. I consider their may be exceptions in some cases for those unlucky ones but I think all this problem of judgement stems from categorizing and catastrophist any subjects you like. In her case, Susans judgements were made by age and appearance of usual participants. Disability is enough despite age or looks we have a lot to prove. Look at Steven Hawking, one of the most intelligent persons, I strongly suspect that people on acquainting even him would maybe talk down to him or in a sympathetic condescending tone.

So truthfully, even I know not the real reason for a majority of behaviour, so comprehend why psychologists and other experts who have studied Disability and societal effects are having troubles imposing a resolve.

I am doing my bit in a community of people that have fathoms to teach.

My bit includes the anti-drunk drive message, if you recoil or utterly do not like the sounds of what we all talk of then don't invite this into personal experience by dangerous driving, drink or drugs or perhaps you think yourself individual and immortal, or that you take things so careful you will make it home. I thought all these things at one stage, let me tell all, if you drink or drug drive destiny is not under your control, I don't have to prove anymore than the honest words I choose, if you refuse advice then you are playing the waiting game. Either law and money and freedom will affect or health and life will. Do you want to die that badly? A night out with mates or on a date is not worth the rest of your life!

You can feel free, do what you like, I did! All the advice and adverts I ignored Really recommend you do not drunk/drug drive or accept a lift in a drink/drug drivers vehicle. Me I would have rather walked home or slept on the path than be a passenger in my car but I had someone who used to get a lift with me after every night out, even at me denying their pleas to stop they still got in the vehicle, thank goodness none of them was so badly hurt as I was. My old self died, not physically but this has taken decades to renew to not yet fully satisfactory levels. Who wants to follow this path, I can safely say no-one and that you're a fool in denial, as I was if you tempt chance. Chances are you will receive your own judgement and have to build a personality and character again. Am not apologizing for my harsh words, I talk from experience, in my talks people need to hear the truth for changes to be made. I have seen change occur in hardened offenders in the one hour presentation, what bewilders me is why all these specialists have not caught on to the blunt truth will redeem, I have seen this.

15- The door is wide - A new inception of disability exclusion and inclusion.

Recall having the thought the door is wide open to those with a new inception of disability exclusion and inclusion. Disability is as individual as we all are and stories although many overlap are to be as singular as the differences in people, everyone has a version of their own discrimination and acceptance, all can make a difference.

The more that give their version and join the movement surely the better equip the whole is to realise appreciate and accept.

Ones mortality faced is I think a strong influencer in affecting relationships between the impaired to the non-disabled, again self preservation is such an all bearing effector to disability integration with society. Most people don't like reminding of how delicate our bodies are, how easily a change to health can massively affect everyday living.

There are specialists who study disability and all associated impositions but personal stories and examples and display, I say from personal experience carry more power to be listened to the the most trained expert. There is something about an audience having more their senses used when learning to make capture of a message more enduring.

I have displayed this and silenced a fidgety hall of students with visual, auditory, emotional, sentimental and personal self-denial factors. The more feeling you can enhance in others the more will be listened to and kept a hold of, people don't have a choice when it comes to differing their ways, the other massive influencer in people is self-preservation, if they don't make the conscious choice they will uncontrollably unconsciously alter their ways and thinking to bring survival inline with what their whole being has witnessed.

Drunk driving and disability go hand in hand with approaches to getting a message heard and also, although I don't want to use disability this is an excellent deferral to drunk drive. All I have said about getting the audience to feel something, as many emotions as possible is made a definite direct fact when self-preservation is made by stories of thinking it was all easy but can lead just as easily to disabilities

16- Intention; - A best society

This book is just part of my efforts for a best society, herein shall discriminate against notable causes. Societal attitudes toward drink driving and disability prejudices.

This will help promote equal treatment and defer drinkers from driving. I have done this myself only after tragic accident survivor became my label do I confuse as to why these messages are so hard to en grain.

I deliver the truth, with upmost honesty, do not care how I may appear to others I have a message or two.

Granted most of society disdain from drink driving and a good majority are not discriminators, but the vast minority and even those good intended at times, due to misinterpreted needs, are still doing both these offences.

I have made hardened offenders cry at realizing what they were tempting so this is why I am sure, you go through all my work and you will never disregard self or others again and if you consider yourself a non-disregarding person this will help toward proper appreciation and consideration.

My life seemed to come to an end although I am determined this is just the beginning of reparation for all.

I have enemies and heroes accompanying me I have spoken about these in my book Drunk drive deterrent, mind travels amid purpose revealed. The words I have utilized at various stages meant these and my work have been faced with mighty barriers, but I will not allow to example as a waste of time, this work has too much prominence.

17- Dont die a fool. The lessons are long and difficult or sudden and devastating.

Ones mortality faced is I think a strong influencer in affecting relationships between the impaired to the non-disabled, again self preservation is such an all bearing affector to disability integration with society. Most people don't like reminding of how delicate our bodies are, how easily a change to health can massively affect everyday living.

There are specialists who study disability and all associated impositions but personal stories and examples and display, I say from personal experience carry more power to be listened to the the most trained expert. There something about an audience having more their senses used when learning to make capture of a message more enduring.

I have displayed this and silenced a fidgety hall of students with visual, auditory, emotional, sentimental and personal self denial factors. The more feeling you can enhance in others the more will be listened to and kept a hold of, people don't have a choice when it comes to differing their ways, the other massive influencer in people is self-preservation, if they don't make the conscious choice they will uncontrollably unconsciously alter their ways and thinking to bring survival inline with what their whole being has witnessed.

Drunk driving and disability go hand in hand with approaches to getting a message heard and also, although I don't want to use disability this is an excellent deferral to drunk drive. All I have said about getting the audience to feel something, as many emotions as possible is made a definite direct fact when self preservation is made use of by stories of thinking it was all easy but can lead just as easy to disabilities

18- An abrupt close
An apt abrupt close, drink/drug-driving/speeding or any

form of dangerous driving will have lasting consequences, quite often an abrupt end of something!

I am a lucky one, yet I know what you are thinking- Want my place?
You are thinking not likely, so you know the answers to that, never, ever think you are invincible or play with lives cos I am sure I dont need to tell ya any more, you will have regrets that equal your biggest mistakes.

Live long in prosperity, dont die a fool.

Feedback is warmly welcomed and replied to;
email;   drivealife@protonmail.com